SOUTHING

SOUTHING

A NOVEL

LILY DARLING

NEW DEGREE PRESS

COPYRIGHT © 2019 LILY DARLING

All rights reserved.

SOUTHING

A Novel

ISBN   978-1-64137-345-6   *Paperback*

          978-1-64137-670-9   *Ebook*

CONTENTS

For Bryer.

"and he says the end isn't always about what dies and I know I know or I knew once and now I write about beautiful things like I will never touch a beautiful thing again"

—HANIF ABDURRAQIB, "AND WHAT GOOD WILL YOUR VANITY BE WHEN THE RAPTURE COMES"

AUTHOR'S NOTE

———

In a café, I read an article about plastics in the ocean and felt sad in a way that I was getting too used to these days.

This is a common experience for kids who grew up in the same time frame as me. Being a New Yorker in a post-9/11 era of climate change, the slogans about polar bears dying and rising sea levels have always been constant background noise. Yes, we know where we are and we know what has to be done. We know the statistics and the names and faces of the people who are destroying our planet. This alone makes it a more existential, certain, threat than anything any other generation has ever faced.

But this is not really that kind of book.

Yes, the idea of this oncoming "climate apocalypse" (or whatever buzzword-friendly headline phrase you might want to use) is a very pressing force throughout this story. However, it is an omnipresent force as well. In this story, it is something that just *is* and has always been—accepted as the fact of the matter and not at all out of the ordinary in the sense that nothing can be done to stop it.

Right now, of course, *absolutely* a lot of things can be done to stop it. In this story it is already too late.

But, again, this is not really that kind of book.

In some ways, this is a book questioning what laws apply in a lawless landscape and the significance of revenge (or, to some, justice) when the cause is already hopeless from its start. It is about a community and the strangers that inhabit it, how their experiences are not neat or simple, but profoundly baroque in a way that is difficult to capture in a few sentences on the page.

Most of all, this is a book about an absence—about the process of mourning and examining what is left behind after the experience of profound loss. This is a story about a missing part of a whole that can never be replaced but can be observed from every angle to the point that it might as well still be there. We love those we have lost so deeply that they continue to breathe in our heads—resurrected by the aftermath and by all they leave behind.

So this story, most of all, is a haunting.

A ghost story.

1.

ATTICUS

It was the fall of San Francisco disappearing into the ocean completely.

The news played footage of it for days on end and spent a whole afternoon premiering a documentary about its history on loop. All those poets and artists, followed by those shabby men and their computers, followed by big men in big suits in tall, tall buildings with too much money. Funny how things can get summed up that quickly.

From their helicopters, they let their cameras roll as the last tower sank below the water, and that was that. Some people cried. Some shared their favorite photos and lit candles in the windows of their homes. Most people just didn't care.

It was also the fall that Mama started slapping Dewey upside the head a lot more often because, they guessed, she was still mad about that time he called her a fat bitch.

Atticus had just started the first grade that month and everything was still hot enough that all the windows had to be open and Mama couldn't make anything in the oven without it getting unbearable. They spent a lot of time outside, so in a way it was like the summer had never ended in the first place. The school days were short, and sometimes Dewey would pick Atticus up in his pretty new car early, so Atticus could do stupid things that would make Dewey and his friends laugh. They liked to hang out under the highway most days. That summer they gave Atticus beer for the first time and made him dance around until he threw up. Well, maybe that wasn't the goal, but that was what happened.

Sometimes Dewey would leave without telling him and Atticus would have to walk home on the side of the interstate by himself. He didn't know if it was okay to do that or not. But a great big part of him wanted Dewey to like him so much it physically hurt, so he didn't say nothing to nobody. He knew as long as he kept his hands in his pockets and his eyes down no one would bother him on those walks back. They were long, but a good portion of it was along the water, which he thought was really pretty to look at.

On Saturday he saw Father Abraham.

They called him Father Abraham because he looked old enough to have been at the founding of Babylon, or something like that. He was a pianist, first. That's what everyone always said. He was a pianist and then he found God during the war. In some stories he was German, in the others he was

French, sometimes—only sometimes—just good old fashioned American. He wore wire-framed glasses and would only stop wandering to deliver a sermon.

It used to be that older kids would drive in their trucks beside him and see how far he could go, but that got boring fast. He just walked, didn't stop for much of anything. Walked like he had everywhere and nowhere to be all at once.

Now, a housewife would sometimes venture out and give him a cup of water on particularly hot days, but that was the extent of the town's interactions with him. The people of Carrabelle didn't know much about how to think about men like him. When he would pass through, people would stop and stare, maybe bring it up in conversation the next day like they would a bout of rain or a brilliant sunrise. He was skeletal, and his skin was browned and freckled by the sun. Only a downy fuzz of white hair dusted his skull, but his eyebrows were thick and his eyelids droopy in nature.

Atticus knelt on the couch with his arms propped against the back cushions to peer out the window as he passed. Mama was smoking a cigarette on their front step and she hesitated for a second as Father Abraham rounded the corner before taking a long pull only to push the smoke back out of the corner of her mouth. Sometimes she would bring the shotgun they kept under the kitchen sink out with her for no reason. Atticus thought it was so none of the neighbors would try and talk to her.

Mama was still wearing her scrubs from work and she had left the TV on with the volume turned all the way up so she could hear it playing through the screen door while she smoked. The lady on the TV was trying to sell a pair of diamond earrings, and it looked like her skin was made of soft paper. Mama's skin crinkled, and she had a mole at the corner of her jaw that she usually covered with makeup. Atticus could tell she was tired because she hadn't covered it that morning, and she had little black smudges under her small eyes.

She took a sip from her coffee as Father Abraham walked past. He walked with his spine curved into itself but each step was just as powerful and smooth as the last, like he knew this was exactly where he needed to be. Even though the lady on the TV was just as loud as she usually was, he made it seem like everything was quiet, that there was only the noise of wind passing through the trees and the humid, humming, heat of a gentle Saturday morning.

Atticus was best friends with a girl who went to the church he preached at two towns over. Her name was Elisa and she knew Atticus better than anyone else in the whole world did. She told him Father Abraham smelled bad but not bad enough that anybody was complaining. She swore that she shook his hand.

Atticus didn't believe her and she knew that, so she really took her time describing everything about Father Abraham. "It was warm but dry," she told him, and Atticus could feel it—like all that sun he soaked up during his wandering decided to stay there a while. Like he was one of those miracle August days when things weren't too humid at all and no one cared about how hot it got because of it. She told Atticus her mama said maybe his walking was something for the soul, like playing the piano or painting a pretty picture. "The only time I saw my daddy cry was when he delivered a sermon after that girl's body was found in the river," she said. "You know, the one who lived close to you."

"Someone should chase him away with a rifle," Dewey said when he looked out the window over Atticus's shoulder. "He ain't human. Swear it."

Atticus told him it wasn't his fault because he couldn't stop walking, even if he tried. Though he never heard that before, he wanted to defend him in some way for some reason. He didn't know why, just felt like he should. Maybe it was something about having respect for a man who could make someone's daddy cry. Maybe that was it.

"It's bullshit," Dewey told him. "The walking. The myths about it or whatever. That's something only horses get." A rot in the liver. Atticus knew. He didn't know how he knew that. He just did. Their next-door neighbor died of the same thing. His cat had eaten a lot of him before someone called the police station complaining about a smell. "Our daddy knew someone during the war that people said the same things about. It's bullshit. That's what he told me, total bullshit."

Atticus didn't believe him. He was always wrong when it came to saying something like that. Dewey always held the words of that ghost like they were a lost sacrament.

That night, Atticus opened all the windows in his room and crawled into bed more tired than he had ever felt before. He stared, out the frame and into the yard as the brush turned into dark shapes etched into a blue-black sky. He closed his eyes and thought he could hear the gentle call of cicadas.

2.

DEWEY

The first time Dewey saw a dead body he was with his daddy.

Atticus—the man, not the boy—had both his hands fixed tightly around the steering wheel as he slammed his foot on the brakes. Dewey was too young to be in the passenger seat, but he was there anyway and just about nearly knocked his teeth out when his daddy stopped the car. He cursed under his breath at the car nearly cleaved in two in the middle of the highway.

That was when they lived in Louisiana.

His daddy loved the water. Wherever they moved, there was always a bayou somewhere. Always mosquitos to slap your neck at.

Dewey don't remember why they were on that road. Don't remember the day or what time it was. It was hot, he knew that because Atticus fanned his face with his hat when he got out of the car to survey the damage.

It wasn't their car, at least he thought. He didn't really know, actually. It wasn't their car, that did that. Whoever it was, they had gone off not that long ago.

There was no smell. That's how he knew. In the summer there was always a smell, even when they killed the chickens. So it must have been fresh, whatever happened.

He remembered looking over the dashboard. Looking at his daddy fan air into his face and run a meaty hand over his sweat-slicked and balding head. He never saw his daddy look like that again. Dewey was too afraid to look at the bodies in the road. But he saw the lower half of one, with its legs bent in a weird way, the rest blocked by the wreck.

Bodies didn't bother him. Growing up he'd killed plenty of chickens, goats, and a pig once too. His daddy taught him how to tape the plastic bags to his feet so he didn't get blood on his boots. How to approach the animal so the meat didn't go fiery—that was the main thing. Atticus always stressed that. You could ruin the meat by scaring the animal. It had to be quick, the first cut. The rest of it was never quick enough, but the first cut had to be. Then once you got the gutting done, the worst of it was over, and that meant dinner wasn't going to be something out of the freezer in the garage that'd been sitting there since last season, all tough and frost-burned. The fresh meat almost made the whole process worth it. Almost.

In Louisiana they had to be self-sufficient like that. Didn't seem hard for Dewey, but his mama was just about ready to bust out of her own skin she was so miserable.

In Florida they were self-sufficient in a ways too, but it took Dewey a lot longer to realize that.

In Florida they went to the supermarket. In Florida there was only one car in the driveway but there was a driveway. They lived off of Johnson's stamps even though mama sneered at them men like him every time he was on the TV.

Didn't need Daddy, even though he'd put a little brother in his mama before he up and left. She named the baby after him even though she hated that man cause she always kept a promise.

She got them a double-wide with an ugly couch and uglier flower-printed wallpaper. She got fat and mean and smoked too many cigarettes working at the senior living complex two towns over.

When Dewey started the seventh grade, they had enough money to move into a house in front of a drainage ditch filled with gators and rotting iguanas. They didn't have enough money to keep the fridge full, but it was a house. He got his own room, got a job doing yard work so he could buy records and then beer for him and his friends. He would go to the grocery store and use his own money to buy him and Atticus dinner for the nights they were on their own.

His best friend Rob gave him one of his old cars as a seventeenth birthday present with the promise that Dewey would be the one to fix it up. He still had issues with the transmission and the trunk had a weird bleach smell to it no matter what he did, but it got girls at school looking at him differently, so he didn't complain. He started calling his mama "Violet" just because it made her mad, especially when she would come home from her shifts tired and cranky. Most days he forgot about his daddy all together.

**

They said when they pulled Jaime's body from the bayou, she was so pale they thought she was one of the roots of the mangroves. Her left arm had been snapped in half. Someone told him it was nearly lopped clean off at the elbow by the time they managed to untangle her. Like the tree didn't want to let go. Like she should have been left to give into the water completely.

When he went to the service—closed casket—and saw the memorial display—her headshot for the yearbook, her smile brilliant—he couldn't help but think of all the time it must have taken to wash the duckweed from her hair. It was black, smooth like a lake at night. He used to sit behind her during American History. She would play with it while she answered the teacher's questions. She always complained that her hands were cold and laughed just a little too loudly whenever someone made a bad joke.

He didn't tell people he went to the funeral. Saw Jaime's mother cry like a dog caught in a fox trap up at the front pew. It looked like she hadn't showered in days and she had big flecks of glitter in her hair. Her skin was leathered by the sun but it still had a sickly quality to it, and she smelled like vodka and vomit. Dewey stayed in the back of the church for pretty much all of it.

There was one time when Violet had Jaime over for dinner. The whole time Dewey could tell that Violet was only doing it as an act of good old Christian charity. It was embarrassingly obvious from the way Violet carried herself around the house while Jaime was there. All "oh yes dear" and "how sweet." Lots of fluttering of the eyes and cruel little smirks at some of the stories Jaime told.

Jaime had been circling Dewey's group of friends at school for a while before that, but Violet only knew of her because Jaime asked her about being a Sunday school teacher. She said she had never read the Bible, but she always wanted to be able to work with little ones.

Violet used to tell that as a funny story whenever they had her friends over for dinner, before Jaime was killed. About that silly little girl who knocked on their door, who said she was good with kids but she'd never gone to a service in her life.

Now, she only told the story of when Jaime asked to be a Sunday school teacher, minus the embarrassing part. Violet said it like she was saying *poor little thing* the whole time.

Usually she would press her hand to her heart when she told that story, like something like that physically hurt, even though she had told it so many times. Dewey didn't know why she kept telling it, even when she knew that—at that point—everyone else damn knew the story. He didn't know why she felt the need to keep talking about it like that.

**

When they pulled Jaime out of the water, she was completely naked. The sheriff on the television said the words "throat" and "ligature" and "no evidence" and "signs of a recent pregnancy," and they went through the town like wind. Like a punch to the gut. Everything was quiet in a real spooky way, even in the days after.

**

Jaime liked to make vases out of clay. She smoked a lot of cigarettes and drank coffee that had too much milk and sugar to be called coffee in the first place. No one knew her mama's name, and she would always pocket extra sandwiches at lunch. Some guy on the football team once paid her fifty bucks so he and his friends could fuck her behind the bleachers after a game. Her clothes were always covered in dust, or paint, or dirt from the community garden that she volunteered at after school.

She had a gap between her two front teeth, a freckle right above her cupid's bow, and a scar on her chin. When Jaime had her "thing" with Dewey's other best friend, Rue, she sat at their table at lunch for a couple of days and told them the story. It was from falling down some metal stairs when she was a kid. She winked at Dewey as she said it, wiping her thumb over the thin white line in one quick and fluid motion.

Dewey sometimes wished he had known her back then. It seemed like maybe things could have been simpler that way.

Simple in the way things were for Atticus. Kinder.

She had this way of describing things, where she would close her eyes and shape whatever it was she was talking about with her hands, like she was trying to conjure it from thin air. It was the most beautiful magic trick he had ever seen.

Rue had shifted uncomfortably when she told that story, even made some kind of a face right at the part where she winked at Dewey. Jaime talked in this way that made it sound like she was flirting with everyone she interacted with. Or maybe she was just a girl who liked to smile a lot and always spoke with her shoulders drawn back and her chin tilted high. It was hard for boys like them to tell the difference, most of the time.

The way she talked made Rue embarrassed, and so they all made fun of her for it. Dewey and Rob, mostly, because they were the defined core of the group, but some of the others made fun of her too. Rue rarely participated but he didn't ask them to stop, either. She didn't sit at their table a while after that.

That was a few weeks before she dropped off the face of the earth. She stopped coming to school completely, only briefly seen in local grocery stores or parks, sometimes with her mother, usually by herself looking tired but refusing to talk to anyone who saw her. That was almost a whole year before they found the body.

Before they found her in the water, Dewey would close his eyes in bed at night and pretend like he would find her hair on his pillow the next morning. He'd hear someone start the shower running in the next room and pretend that she was in there. And they were alone, and they had nothing but time to pull the sheets around them and become some type of ghost.

Her name was Jaime. Sounded like it was made to be said softly. Jaime.

**

When he held a body under his own for the first time, he thought he would close his eyes and imagine her because everyone was still mourning like it had just happened yesterday, the whole county it felt like. A sadness, a quiet that stretched over the whole of everything he walked through. Violet whispered about it with her friends in their pastels at church.

Sometimes, only sometimes, people would talk about the crushed skull, the broken bones, the destroyed house that signaled something long and messy and too slow. Too slow.

When he fucked someone for the first time, he really thought he would close his eyes and think of Jaime's living mouth. But, instead, he couldn't help but notice how the girl's heart beat like it was up and trying to leave her ribcage. How big her eyes were when she looked up at him, like he was something else, someone else.

It made him feel strong. Made him feel like the wrought-iron straps of muscle that corded his father's forearms.

The girl's name—the one he kissed, not the one in the dirt—was Carol Anne. She had brown eyes and hair she dyed blonde herself because she wanted to be like the girls with leather headbands and puka necklaces they saw on TV. Her family didn't go to church, he knew that much. And she acted mean and cold, but when he put his arm over her shoulders at Rob's pool party, she got real quiet—a soft kind of quiet—and she smiled a lot more.

"You can stop calling me that, you know," she told him. "Callie is fine."

"Callie?" They were in Rob's kitchen. It was too loud outside to hold a conversation and Rob had broken Dewey's nose for no other reason than it was a Saturday night and they were drunk, so he was holding a bag of frozen peas to his face. He should have felt ridiculous, but he didn't for some reason.

Rob's guard dog had pressed himself against Dewey's leg and was licking the blood off his hand.

Rob's dad had gotten the thing as a gift when he went to Armenia for some kind of business trip. Rob told Dewey more than once that it creeped him out but he didn't ask any questions. It came up to Dewey's hip and had a thick coat of black fur hiding an even thicker layer of muscle.

Annabelle named it Button and used to knot the fur at the top of its head with a little bow when she was still in middle school. Dewey thought Button was kind of sweet in a dopey way before he saw it eviscerate a neighbor's escaped terrier in less than ten seconds. Then it made sense that Rob called Button his "little wolf killer" whenever they got drunk, and Dewey had to start pretending not to be terrified of the thing.

The girl, Callie, started laughing when the dog lapped at Dewey's fingers, muttering, "That's so fucked up," under her breath. He was drunk enough now to just laugh along with Callie at the licking, and he didn't even realize he'd started to scratch the top of its head.

The speakers that were probably worth more than Dewey's car were playing some song with too much bass and a lot more yelling. The lights were low, and Callie had pushed herself onto the island's counter so she was just over eye level with him. She smiled, her teeth looking whiter in the dim light.

"Yeah, Callie."

"Well it's a real pleasure, Callie."

She laughed, something bright. He remembered in English class an author describing a girl's laughter like a peal of bells. He understood that now. Peal of bells. That's what it was.

"You from around here?"

"Yeah. Since I was a kid."

When she nodded, it was like she was bobbing her head to the music drifting in from outside. She tucked a frizzy wave of brown-blonde hair behind her ear as she did. "Cool, cool. I uh, just moved here. Well—like, a few months ago, actually. But I still feel new. You get it?"

"Yeah I get it." He swirled the cup in his hand, a dark brown mix of liquors that made his throat burn. "Where were you from before?"

"A town outside of Richmond, but my dad moves around a lot for his work."

The rumor was they had to get out of town because her brother was a faggot. Said he was sleeping with a teacher and it ruined her daddy's whole career. Dewey didn't tell her that everyone already knew that though. "That's cool, real cool."

"My brother's in your grade. He told me you're dropping out next year."

"Yeah." The top of him felt heavier than the rest. Something about an ache in his gums. It felt good to run his hand over the top of the dog's head, the repeated motion of it. "One of Mr. Fairchild's old friends has a job for me out west on one of those corporate farms. The pay is better than anything down here." He could have said something about wanting to stay, a part of him wanting to watch out for Atticus, that all they had was each other and those TV dinners, but he did not know that yet.

She nodded, her upper lip bulging slightly as she ran her tongue over her front teeth. She looked nervous, like she wanted to ask something she knew she shouldn't. There was a brief silence that should have been awkward if he were sober enough to care. "Isn't that gonna be hard?"

"Huh?"

"Workings fields, with the droughts and all that?" She shrugged. "I dunno, just from what I've seen in the news and shit. Seems pretty awful." All the news had been showing lately was reels of dead soil and mud slides and men with callused hands and dust-beaten skin in white masks. Whatever it meant, it was easier than the slaughterhouse Rue was going to have to go to. Corn was easier to deal with than meat, easy as that. "I'm surprised he didn't just get you some kind of job at one of the clinics is all, you know?"

"You just burn shit and start over. Seems pretty simple to me," Dewey said. He ran his tongue over his teeth. He realized she started to speak faster the closer he got to her. He didn't think he'd ever made someone like that before. "Plus, they're building all those greenhouses now. Don't even need natural air anymore."

She looked like she didn't agree, but she didn't say any-thing. "I'm pretty sure Mr. Fairchild's trying to move all that stuff to the northeast, you know?" She was talking about the clinics. "Everything's way worse up there." Not nearly true. Dewey couldn't drive home from school without seeing some poor shit overdosing on the side of the highway, but what Callie said was what Rob kept repeating to them. "But at least the weather is nicer. Almost no fires and the flooding isn't that bad yet."

Dewey shrugged.

"Rob told me you were gonna be lookin' over the house while they go up to New York?"

Callie smiled. "Yeah, Mr. Fairchild wanted someone to look after that little guy while they got settled." She nodded toward Button. Dewey patted its head twice before switching the hand he was using to hold the peas against the throb-bing side of his face. Half the house was already packed in moving boxes, though there wasn't much stuff to ship off in the first place.

"Weird to think about them leaving and all." Rob threw his "end of the fucking world" party for two reasons—tomor-row's eclipse and the excuse to have a "final hurrah." He told Dewey this while they were all drunk on Rue's roof. Rob had pushed the handle of vodka they were sharing into the air as he said it, saluting the moon, and then threw his head back and laughed. What this town was going to be without the

Fairchilds was an important question, why they were leaving not necessarily certain.

"Business is business, I guess." Callie shrugged.

Dewey gave her a low kind of smile. "You're not wrong." He asked her if she wanted to talk someplace quieter.

**

They fucked on a green velvet couch in the basement. It was dusty and the whole room smelled like a thrift shop, but it felt nice. Nice how a dog might feel lying in the sun, or cold water hitting the back of your throat on a hot day. Nice in a surreal kind of way.

Later, when he could only keep his eyes open for the sake of stopping the world from spinning, she asked him if he knew the girl. *Jaime.* She said her name like it was a secret. He said he didn't. He said his friends went to watch as they pulled her out of the water. He said he heard the funeral reception was real pretty.

3 .

NEWBURY

———

Newbury left his house for the last time a week ago.

He promised himself the clothes on his back and the food in his stomach and that was just about it. He bought a car from a man he met on the side of the road who told him his brother had died. The man was older, skin leathered and dry, stretched around knobby joints that moved like they didn't want to. He wore an army jacket and cargo shorts. Newbury had complimented him on his shorts. He didn't know why he did because he thought they were very ugly.

The man said a house fire killed his brother and that the car was all that was left. He said he wanted to get rid of the car so nothing was left. Newbury understood that part more than anything else.

Four hours outside of Basalt he got caught in the rain. It started slowly, and he thought the sound of water against his windshield was just a part of the radio broadcaster's voice. *He is talking about the moon*, Newbury thought. It sounded distant, like someone else was walking through his head, trying to tell him something important. *He is talking about the moon and something much bigger than I will ever be. Bigger than anyone will ever be.* In the wind, the grass moved like a human might.

When Newbury was young, he would stand in the rain with his hands raised as if he could control it. He would scream to the clouded skies, gray-black with thunder and the smell of ozone. His clothes would become a second skin, slicked to his body. Newbury felt like he knew how someone somewhere sometime was able to dream of werewolves and turn it into a legend that transcended time. This unearthly feeling clawing its way through his throat was like something trying to get him to strip off his skin and run.

He hadn't felt that feeling in a long time. He knew this, staring out the parked car's windshield at the grass that whipped in the wind like children playing in a storm.

He hid from the rain. The suit he bought with the remaining money in his bank account hugged his shoulders a little too tightly. He had eggs and toast and a cup of coffee for five dollars in a roadside diner, and the florescent bulbs had let out an unending wail of desperation. The waitress wore a pretty perfume. She made a joke about how he should wash his hair and he thought he laughed at it. She gave him a second cup of coffee for free.

Newbury stayed there a long time, so she told him there was an elk on the interstate that morning after she'd dropped her little girl off for school. Traffic and everything had completely stopped to let him pass. She said it got real quiet, too. That even though people around here went and shot at them on the weekends all the time, this morning they were real quiet. She said it was like watching a ghost pass as it wove its way between the cars—or a God, with antlers as big as that. She said the sight of those things alone sucked the air right out of her chest. She described it as a "thorny veil." As she said that she brought both her hands up to the sides of her head and wiggled her fingers like she was telling a scary story to a little kid.

The coffee tasted better then. The rain had stopped and he sat in the booth and made sure to take really small sips so he still had an excuse to stay there a while longer. At one point the kind waitress asked him if he had somewhere to go and he said yes. She looked surprised by that.

She asked him where he was from. He said his grandfather was from Argentina and his mother's family was from Taiwan. She laughed and rolled her eyes and said, "No, not like *that*. I mean where did your mother raise you?" She was wearing a turquoise nail polish that made her skin look like chalk. Or maybe it was the florescent lights.

"Metairie. Right outside of New Orleans," he said the name like his city was still there. Like it was something he could get up and walk to at any second, like it wasn't all just water and salt now. The waitress let out a low whistle.

"I'm real sorry about that."

"Yeah." That was all he could say. He didn't know why. He sometimes thought that maybe the grass deserved that land back. All that swamp and mud had been wanting those cities for centuries. It was only right. It was only right.

"I had family in Long Island," the waitress took out a napkin and started cleaning the table. It looked like she just wanted to do something with her hands. "They were sent to those evac campuses out here in Colorado. Had to make it there themselves. Weren't even promised a space until they got there. Sounded like hell on earth, just awful."

Newbury had lived in New York for a long time. He wanted to be a poet, but he wasn't any good at it. He almost got married to a girl with deep brown skin and wide eyes.

When he first met her at a college party, she smelled like flavored liquor and burnt paper. Her mouth tasted like rotted fruit and coffee. She made fun of him when he mentioned that his dad used to be a cop.

She said she liked the way his voice sounded when they shared a cigarette outside. She unzipped his coat in that cold November air, pressed her ear against his chest, and told him to say something. His heart beat so fast. She pressed her hand against his ribs and smiled up at him because only then did she realize how nervous he was.

She lived in a studio apartment with a fat cat. Sometimes he had dreams where he woke up and was back there, in her bed, staring out the window that opened onto a fire escape. The couple who lived next door would fight so loudly it would sometimes wake them up. She would roll over and turn on the radio to drown out the screaming. He swore the shapes the shadows made on her skin as she moved were something that would be engrained in his memory forever, even though he had already forgotten her name.

"Yeah," he said again. He looked into his coffee, wishing he had brought enough money to tip. He wanted to tell her about New York. About Louisiana and his mother's home. Growing up in the slick southern heat. His father's calloused hands. His best friend, Warren, and the rain. The move west and the job at the police station that made him miss a home he had never had.

She took away his plate. He wanted her to tell him more about the elk, about how the trees sounded in its presence.

"Where are you headed to?" She filled his coffee up again, even though he wasn't done with it.

He told her he was going to visit an old friend before he got re-enlisted to work as a roughneck on an oil rig off coast. She got a different look in her eyes after that. She told him she hoped he had a really good day. She stopped refilling his cup.

An older man, seated behind Newbury, scoffed the third time the waitress walked pass them without so much as a glance in Newbury's direction. He was very fat and red in the face and had his cane laid across the seat opposite to him. "Fuckin' environmentalists," the man said to either the air or Newbury, Newbury wasn't sure. "Don't know how grateful they should be for men like us."

Newbury thought the cruelty in the man's voice made him get up and leave so quickly. It made him feel like all the skin on the back of his neck was made of crumpled up aluminum foil, and he suddenly realized how bright the lights were. He needed to get *out* before anyone realized how he didn't have any money left in any of his pockets and—

Once he was back in the car, he had to keep both hands wrapped tightly around the wheel to keep himself from eating the bottle of pills in the glove compartment. Two nights prior, he had swallowed one and it had turned into a swarm of mites that crawled out of his throat. He spent the entire evening on the bathroom floor crying and trying to spit them out.

**

When they were younger than they were now   younger as in not in the ground, for Warren, younger as in clear-headed and sound, for Newbury—the two of them would spend hours driving in their fathers' cars because that was the only thing kids had to do back then. Newbury remembered being behind the wheel, having taken the roof off the old Jeep, and Warren stood up and stuck his head out the window and just screamed. He just screamed.

When they were even younger than that, Newbury and Warren would spend hours in the woods pretending to hunt the animals their fathers did on the weekends. They set up traps that didn't work made of branches lashed together with the twine their mothers used to cook chicken with.

When the fires started, the clouds would turn purple-yellow at night. There was so much ash in the air the moon looked orange. It was pretty, but the wind carried this smell, and the sky had these undertones of green all the time. Warren said it looked like the bruises his daddy would get working in the yard all week. Warren said his ma would make a juice from the earth to put over them to help with the ache.

Warren's ma never trusted nothing from the drug stores—not since Warren's baby sister was killed because one of the big companies that took over all the doctors' offices in Louisiana gave her the wrong medicine for her cough that started because of the fires. Newbury forgot which company, but he knows it was the same one that also started supplying the old FEMA tents that molded too easy once the flooding started.

**

Newbury kept driving until it felt like he was only lungs. Manic. Heart beating so fast he had to pull over to the shoulder of the road just to keep his vision from doubling anymore. He couldn't stop thinking about the story of the elk.

Or maybe it was the ugly purple faces of the mountains as the sun began to creep over the horizon again. Or maybe it was the panic of not realizing that the sun had set and the sky had blackened for however long enough for the sun to rise again. Or maybe it was the waitress's turquoise fingernails and the crooked teeth she spoke through.

He wanted to ask her about her daughter, to imagine a world where she didn't get so afraid after he told her about going off coast. He wanted to have turned around and told that old man that almost every roughneck was an ex-con drug addict anyway so she had the right to act that way and then maybe force the man's head on the table until he turned into something else.

He wanted to be able to tell her that sometimes he had dreams where he was in a boat with Warren, and the water beneath them was all oil, heavy with the weight of its own sick, rainbow body. And Warren kept filling cups of it for him to drink, and Newbury was always worried he would fall in if he leaned over the side of the boat. He knew Warren wanted him to drink. All of it. To become full. And the sun was such a brilliant shade of red—

Newbury blinked his eyes open and he was in front of a motel. His chest was quiet. His thoughts were clear and sharp as a bird's song.

He got out of the car. He had sunglasses now. He didn't know how they got there but he was thankful for them in the swampy heat.

The motel sat stout and crumbling by the side of the road. The neon sign was turned off, but the piece of paper taped on the clerk's window said there was a vacancy. The asphalt was shattered with weeds stretching through the cracks that had blistered and coiled in the wet heat of the sun. The sky was a pure type of blue. The highway was lined with wilted palmettos.

The photos in his back pocket, a reminder.

Florida, yes.

The weight pressing down on his ribs, a kind of anger that took the air right out of you.

The girl.

He knew it was the right place. He stepped inside.

4.

CALLIE

Callie lied to Dewey. Many times. Fully. Right through her teeth. More than she should have. More than she would be able to keep up with, she realized, as she snuck out of Rob's house through the back door before the sun broke the hazy horizon. Her car was parked on the lawn of the neighbor's house. Annabelle, her best—and only—friend, said it would be okay because their neighbors' kids only used that house for parties anyway.

Callie had never seen someone enter or exit any other home in Annabelle's cul-de-sac. Sometimes different cars would be parked briefly in different driveways, but the boxwood gave everyone an iced-out sense of secrecy—the cold shoulder with nothing welcoming about a solid wall of green.

She used to have a lot more friends like Annabelle. She used to go to a boarding school in Virginia—a big private school with wrought iron gates, a great lawn, and uniforms with little black shoes and white stockings. Maywich. The name alone dripped hedge funds and questionable family histories. She learned quickly to keep this from people once they moved. There was no room in a place like Carrabelle for prep-school girls with once-rich daddies. Understandable.

Annabelle and Rob Fairchild reminded her a lot of her friends at home, too much so sometimes. Those kids of movie-stars and politicians. Now she had to pretend to not know her own family's name at school. They registered her under her mother's maiden name "for safety purposes." Bullshit, but whatever. It was a quick adjustment, but it had her feeling uneasy for some time after.

Before Beau ran away, she at least used to have a pair of understanding eyes to link with over the dining room table. Now there was only an empty seat.

Sometimes, just sometimes, she wished she could go back in time to when she was so small she needed help with everything in the world. Back to when he would hold her hand when they walked from their house to the playground and he would kick stones over so they could pick through the worms and grubs living underneath. She couldn't say what changed, but it did. And that was that.

**

The night before, when Dewey had kissed her, his nose had been broken so bad his blood got in her mouth.

It was the Fairchild's party. Well, it was Rob's party really, but Annabelle decided to play the "I'm in high school now too" card, which was strategically followed up by, "If you don't let me go, I'm telling Dad you've been stealing his coke," and so Rob begrudgingly let his baby sister invite a few friends over too.

Callie had tried to straighten her hair for the party but the humidity outside decided against it. She tugged on a pair of skinny jeans before she left the house and borrowed a white tube top from Annabelle's closet. Fidgeting with her makeup in the mirror, Annabelle told Callie that these boys had no idea who Beau was, even though they were in the same class.

Callie got really close to saying she didn't really want to hear anything about her runaway shitbag of a brother, but Annabelle said it in a way that sounded like she was trying to be nice. So Callie just shrugged instead.

Mr. Fairchild was upstairs, but she promised he wouldn't come down because he was cool like that. Annabelle then made a comment how maybe Callie should buy a flat iron from the pharmacy or something. Annabelle said she could send Callie one from Macy's because she, her dad, and Rob were all moving to New York soon. After all, they had all sorts of sales for stuff like that up there because that's where all the models lived.

"Maybe," Annabelle said. "Maybe I'll become a model. How cool would that be? I could buy you a plane ticket and you could come visit me whenever you wanted."

Callie told her she liked that idea.

She went to the bathroom and put her hair in a bun.

Rob and Dewey and Rue came in a Firebird convertible, the kind Beau had wanted after he got his first job sophomore year at the furniture shop in town. But their dad refused to get Beau one because he had this whole thing about "building character."

The trio and two others Callie had never seen before were piled into a two-seater, racing down the street with the top down and the radio on full blast. Dewey was in the driver's seat with two friends squeezed beside him. The girl was stuck in the middle with her knobby legs over the stick shift.

One of the friends sitting behind them, the one on the headrest with his legs straddling her shoulders, made a crude joke about it as they walked into Annabelle's house. The girl laughed and slapped his arm. She had a tattoo on the joint of her thumb and hair cut to her sharp jaw. She told Callie later that she had lived in France with her mother last year. She said the coffee was better there, "But the men are still pigs, so that's not much of a change." Callie forgot her name.

They stayed in Annabelle's backyard with the drained pool, the potted plants, and the glass table littered with beer cans.

The eclipse was happening tomorrow and people were kind of losing their minds about it. For weeks there had been evangelical preachers proselytizing in the streets. End times, they said. God taking back what was his. Fire and brimstone, horses and pale riders and the sun blinking out of existence forever. Lots of people had convinced themselves it was the beginning of the end, and the Fairchild siblings, Rob and Annabelle--but mostly Rob--were using it as an excuse to throw a party big enough to have had the entire school buzzing about it for days beforehand.

Rob and his two best friends, Rue and Dewey, were virtually inseparable. Annabelle always called them the "chaos trio," usually paired with some kind of a scoff or vicious eye roll. But Callie could tell by the way her voice shifted an octave whenever they were around that she was just as intimidated by their combined premise as Callie was.

Rob and all of them really reminded her of the pack of dogs that had been in street in front of her Sunday school teacher's home when she was young. They had nipped at each other's throats and seemed to travel as a mass of tawny limbs, yipping and growling and pouncing forward to some unseen chaotic horizon. They were joyful and fearsome and all gnashing teeth as the neighborhood looked through parted curtains and anxiously held back sons and daughters from the toys scattered across front lawns as the dogs capered through the streets.

In the heady September darkness, under the sparse fairy lights strung across the backyard, every head was thrown back in laughter, every movement of the body set to the pounding rhythm of the guitar looked like a tiny exorcism. Every can raised high into the air toasting to "the end of the fucking world" was met with howls of approval.

Callie and Annabelle had to pool together money and use Annabelle's older sister's ID to get those three boxes of beer, each from three different gas stations. Rob had asked them to. Annabelle pretended not to be nervous in the car, but her voice warbled the whole time she talked to the cashier. When Annabelle slipped back into the car, she said that if Beau hadn't up and left "like that," he could have gotten it for them. Callie had a weird feeling in her throat until they got back to the house after that.

The first thing he said to her was, "Could you turn the music up?"

Dewey said this, not the now absent brother.

He looked her right in the eyes and gave a half smile with one corner of his mouth. She froze for a moment and then nodded. She turned to kneel in front of the speakers, her molars warm from the drink she placed on the ground next to her.

The music was something with an oppressive amount of bass and very little lyrics. The trio liked listening to their dads' kind of music. They knew if they put on anything recent, the energy would go down fast. Rob was the gatekeeper of what seemed to be an infinite supply of bottles from his father's medicine cabinet, so all of Annabelle's friends who were there learned fast to keep quiet and just nod along.

Dewey thanked her and there was this silent moment.

There was this silent moment.

He reached above her head and before she knew it, his fingers undid her hair tie without any of the curls knotting around the band at all. Her shoulders were covered by waves of unruly brown-blonde and that silence was fluid. And perfect. It felt like the breath was knocked out of her, and it felt like a movie or one of those bad romance novels she would glance through at the bookstore but never buy for fear of her cheeks turning too red at the register.

He said he liked her hair. She kept her face turned away and gave him a quiet, "Thank you." Her mother's earrings pressed against her cheek and the silence remained unbroken as he slipped past her.

A blur settled over all them. Callie lost track of how many new faces she saw. Songs blended into each other. Three hours felt like three minutes, and three minutes felt like three hours. She thought she might have made friends with a sophomore who was holding another girl's hair back in the bathroom but forgot about the experience completely as soon as she stumbled back outside. The boys talked in their loud voices interspersed with bright tinkling laughter from Annabelle and that French girl. Callie smiled along with them even when she couldn't understand what they were saying.

It was almost 1 a.m. when Rob punched Dewey in the mouth.

He fully broke Dewey's nose. Callie could have sworn she heard the crunch of it and everything. She was walking by right as it happened and Dewey almost fell right on her.

And then there was this moment when everyone else was still. Rob, standing over Dewey's crumpled body in both awe and horror, had his fists clenched at his side. Annabelle, mouth open and eyes wide, froze in place. The French girl rested her elbow against her knee with the cigarette clamped between her ring and middle finger. And the music, the bass grating and loud and swarming into every nervous fiber swarmed around Rob's fists as they clenched and loosened. Clenched and loosened.

Less than ten minutes ago, Rob and Dewey had their arms around each other's shoulders and their foreheads pressed together to howl the lyrics to some Otis Redding song that her mother hated, just centimeters away from kissing, and now they were here. Dewey blinked both his eyes open and rolled onto his side and muttered something like, "Fuck, man."

Callie was closest to Dewey when it happened, so she stepped forward and extended her arm to help him up. He took it after a moment of holding his face with both hands. He mumbled, "Fuck," again and stumbled a bit. Callie caught him with a hand pressed against his stomach and the other pressed against his ribs. He was skinny and tall enough that she had to tilt her head back a bit to look him in the eye.

"Are you okay?" she asked, quickly pulling her other hand away and only leaving one steadying palm on his bicep.

Dewey made a sharp, strangled noise and spat on the ground. "What the fuck do you think?"

Rue shouted something about ice being in the kitchen and then went back to talking to the girl sitting on his lap. His voice broke the stunned silence and everyone went back to what they were doing, only giving Dewey and her side-long glances from where they were huddled in their little groups around the backyard.

"Through those doors." Dewey nodded in their direction. "Fuck, I think he hit my eye or something." A bloody film turned his teeth an orange color. He had some of his own spit coming out of the corner of his mouth.

Later, in the kitchen, she remembered drunkenly pressing two fingers against the swollen bump. The only thing they could find was a bag of frozen peas to press against the left side of his face, so he held it there the entire time they talked.

She had tried to wipe away most of the blood with a wet paper towel, and in her haze curiously reached up and prodded at the bump that was beginning to form. He'd hissed and whacked her hand away while grimacing, and she had apologized. He laughed and *kissed* her and pulled her into his chest.

Callie was fifteen and the saddest she thought she might have ever been and her hands started getting shaky when he pressed his forearm against the cabinets above her head and leaned in to kiss her harder. Then he got his blood in her mouth, but she didn't mention it because she was so surprised by the kiss in the first place.

**

During the one church service she went to when they first got to Florida, she watched her mother drink a Dixie cup of wine that was supposed to be the blood of Christ.

This was supposed to demonstrate her love for him.

The woman behind them was still crying as Callie's mother wiped at the corners of her mouth with the hand-kerchief from her purse.

**

She had known of Dewey before the party. They all went to the same high school, and he was her best friend's brother's best friend, after all. Annabelle told Callie that he had been kind of friends with that girl, the one who was killed, but she knew they weren't close or anything. This was before the party, before Dewey took her hair tie and got his nose broken and kissed her like *that* in the kitchen.

Annabelle told her about Dewey and *that girl* at lunch while they were sharing a cigarette on one of the benches near the art studio building. It was a few days after they had found the body, and everyone numbly kept going about their business. It seemed like there was no excuse to weep openly anymore.

"Must be weird coming into all this and have no idea what's going on," Annabelle said as she exhaled. She was wearing a light blue tank top and a white denim skirt. Some of the ash from the cigarette had fallen onto her thigh but she hadn't noticed it yet. "Not to be that bitch, but none of these fuckers gave a shit about her when she was still alive." She extended the cigarette to Callie with a languid flick of her wrist.

"Jesus, Annabelle," Callie took it anyway. They could see Rob and his friends at their usual spot from where they were standing. "Maybe wait another, like, seventy-two hours before you start saying stuff like that."

"What?" Annabelle scoffed, tucking a strand of thick black hair behind her ear and crossing her legs. She was wearing her mother's Chanel espadrilles and had been complaining all day about the blisters they were giving her. "Listen, she was friends with my brother. I can say shit like that if I want to. I actually knew the damn chick."

"She was friends with Rob?"

"Yeah," Annabelle said as she narrowed her eyes. Her sweat and the mascara she wore had left two identical little arcs on her under eyes and she had put concealer that didn't quite match her skin tone on a zit at the lower corner of her lip. She was thin in the way that you could start to see the notches of her trachea, but she was tan and smiled enough that nobody worried about her. "That's the chaos trio—Rob and Rue and Dewey." She nodded with her chin toward their table. "Dewey was kind of obsessed with her but he thinks no one knows that. It was totally obvious from the start."

Dewey had one of his arms draped over Rue's shoulders and they were talking about something quietly. Or maybe no one was talking and Dewey was just nodding his head slowly to the music one of them was playing from their shitty phone speakers.

They had their table—Rob, Rue, and Dewey. And it was known as "their" table. It was one of a handful of picnic benches in the field area where they could take their lunches if it wasn't too hot outside. It *was* too hot, and the sky was this muggy kind of rolling gray. They were all just waiting for the next clap of thunder to go back inside.

This was one of the few times during the day they could get away from the teachers because Mr. Peterson didn't give a shit and would just peek out the little window in his office in the gym that overlooked the field sometimes to make sure no one was skipping class or smoking pot or anything even though he'd copped from Rob on multiple occasions.

Mr. Peterson generally didn't give a shit about a lot of things. That's why most of the kids liked him. His wife left him and took their dog. Left the kid but took the dog. Or, that's what most of the rumors said anyway.

Rue had his head on the table and Annabelle told Callie he was still pretty torn up about the whole "dead girlfriend thing." But she put "girlfriend" in air-quotes and rolled her eyes in a way that told Callie Annabelle thought he was another one of the people who was using this whole ordeal as an excuse to cry in public.

Dewey was a junior and had dark hair that just brushed his jawline and a smattering of freckles over his nose. He didn't have much to say at all and seemed to be too good at shutting down conversations before they could even be started. He came into school drunk most days. Or angry.

He looked up from where he was comforting Rue, over the shoulder of his worn band shirt, and seemed to look right at Callie and Annabelle like he knew they were talking about him. But Callie was good at knowing when she was getting looked at versus looked through. She looked back anyway.

ABBOT, PISCATAQUIS COUNTY

The innkeeper flipped through the pages of the newspaper, eyes barely passing over the articles detailing the nor'easter that would be passing through that weekend. She kept the prosthetic arm leaning against the table, the working hand pinching the corners of the pages to turn to the next story.

The headliner was a story about the first solar eclipse in thirty-two years that was supposed to happen the next day. The pull-quote said something about the moon's retreating orbit, the final chance of witnessing "totality" for the next seventy-something years.

She liked that word, totality. There was something so dramatic about it—very final in its nature, almost like a goodbye. In a sense, it was going to be.

Her mother, sleeping upstairs, had an old TV drama playing at a volume high enough that she could catch a word or two in Farsi. Someone's wife was dead—or cheating—or pretending to have died to cheat on another man. She wasn't sure, but the hum helped with the monotony of staring outside the window to the bleak dark clouds, the highway, and the field their house rested on. It drowned out the sound of the breathing machine and the heart monitor with its constant chatter.

The cars on the highway rushed past with headlights blaring.

The door was pushed open by a rain-slicked couple—two men, both wearing windbreakers with the hoods pulled over their heads. Only one of them pulled his down. The other, the one carrying a baby, stayed standing by the door, the upper half of his pale face hidden. He held the child in a way that looked like he'd never held a kid before, nervously bouncing it up and down, with one hand cupping the back of its neck and the other pressing its body to his wet chest. Her eyes slid back to the man who approached her warily.

He pulled out a wallet from his back pocket. "How much for one night?" His eyes flicked down to the prosthetic briefly, before moving back up to her face.

She straightened, closing the newspaper. "Fifty. Cabins include a kitchen and bathroom."

"Cash okay?" He was leafing through some crumpled up bills in his wallet. He had no cards. His head was shaved, and he had a tattoo on his left cheek too old and poorly done to make anything of it than a blue-black smudge, like he got pen on his face and his mother had tried to get it off by licking her thumb and dragging it downward.

"If it's all you got," she eyed his partner from over his shoulder. "Your buddy over there doing alright?"

He turned his head and a neck tattoo peeked above the collar of his jacket. "How you doin', Shug?"

The other man's voice was quiet. "I'm fine."

Face-tattoo gave her a straight-toothed grin. His teeth were too big for his mouth. "Just dandy, see?" He slid 250 dollars in damp dollar bills across the table. "Is there a problem?"

She remembered the breathing machine upstairs, a pile of bills unpaid, and the nurse hired to watch her mother's heart patter on a screen all night.

The innkeeper looked at the money and then looked at the man, half bent cockily over her desk. The murmuring from upstairs wasn't so loud anymore, somehow drowned out by the presence of the men in the room.

"And what brings a Southern gentleman like you up here?" She tried not to sound too interested. "I thought Maine was a little too cold for folks like you."

"We worked lumber up in Uvalde, got pushed out by the fires." She knew he was lying by how smooth it sounded. Or maybe she was just paranoid. "Looking for work up here while that plays itself out."

"I like the trees," his partner's voice was so soft it almost frightened her. "They're beautiful up here."

She barked out a genuine laugh at that. "A lumberman that likes trees. Christ, okay. Okay." The register had a hard time opening, so she had to punch in the total twice before the drawer slid open. The guest with his forearms against the table looked like he was having a hard time containing his anger at his partner's comment.

The smaller man, Shug, presumably, continued. "In the fires, the sky was always purple at night. Even in the place we were staying. There was so much ash in the air it turned the sky a bruised purple, and the moon was orange. It was pretty, but the wind carried this smell, and the sky had these undertones of green." He had a way of both completing a sentence and leaving it hanging half finished, not necessarily a question or a statement. Not dreamy, but soft. And somehow with this she believed them—him, really. There was a fire. They were meaning to escape a home and find something someplace else.

His partner tapped his fingers against the counter, jolting her back to cautious suspicion.

"So how about those room keys?" The man smiled and it was a wolf's grin.

5.

ATTICUS

———

On Sundays, Mama would make him breakfast before they went to services.

Atticus liked the ritual of it, laying out his clothes on the blue dresser the night before, waking up nearly before the sun rose because if he got up early enough, she would let him have a small cup of coffee because she always accidentally made too much. It made him feel adult, like maybe how Dewey felt getting back late at night all the time and driving his own car and everything.

Sometimes Dewey would stay out so late that he came back home when Atticus started getting ready for school. Dewey would sneak back into his room through the back door and Atticus would make enough noise fixing his breakfast that Mama wouldn't catch on—or, at least he tried to. Lots of slamming cabinets and shaking of the cereal box.

He was stuck between trying to make Dewey like him and making his mama happy a lot. Sometimes he felt like the little things mattered the most, even though it didn't seem like either of them noticed much of anything.

He woke up that Sunday covered in sweat, the little fan propped by the window motionless. The power must have gone out. The sky was an inky kind of blue that meant the sun was going to rise soon.

He pulled his pillow off the bed and walked to the living room. It was cooler on the floor, and he could open the sliding doors to the backyard for more air.

Mama liked to keep their yard wild. A pack of wild boars would sometimes drift through and dig up the crabgrass, and countless tadpoles lived in the hollows created by the rain. Mama said that the day they brought him home from the hospital she saw a flock of flamingos fly right over them. She said that was as good a sign as any. As soon as she saw "them birds," she knew they were right where they were supposed to be.

Sometimes when he went into the living room, Dewey would already be asleep on the couch. He would have the trashcan pulled up next to him and he usually smelled like moldy bread and something more bitter. On those mornings Atticus would put his pillow on the floor next to the couch and sleep there instead, even though the carpet made his whole body itch.

Once the sun rose on mornings like that, Mama would wake him up, yell at Dewey for a bit, and force him into the shower. Mama and Dewey usually got into a fight over Dewey taking his own car to church because Dewey would say he wanted to listen to his own music and Mama would say something like, "How would it look to my friends if I can't even get my own son to ride to service with me?"

Dewey wasn't there that morning, though. Mama kept glaring at the couch he was usually sprawled across like he would suddenly appear there so she could finally speak her mind at him.

Atticus thought the quiet was nice. He got up off the floor, got dressed, and ate the waffle Mama made him so fast it made his stomach hurt something mean. At one point, when they were putting their dishes away, Mama ruffled the top of his hair and told him he looked very handsome. Atticus scrunched his face up at that.

Their church was nice and looked a whole lot like it was older than Carrabelle itself. It was held up by thick sandstone bricks and he could see one of the gargoyles—its face twisted in a snarl like the cartoons on TV—from where they parked their car every Sunday.

Mama liked to be old fashioned and she said all the new Churches they put up creeped her out. That the air conditioning was always too cold and the preachers too "young looking." This was also the church all her friends went to, so there was that, too.

Atticus liked it because of the gardens out back. They had a running stream with koi fish and everything. The Sunday school teacher told him it was a place to go so he could think, if he ever needed that, which Atticus thought was a nice thing to tell someone.

That morning, they started singing during the services and it felt like his chest was trying to tear itself apart. It suddenly got really hard to breathe, so he got up and walked right out the door. He didn't know why. He just left.

Mama was busy whispering to one of her friends, and the preacher was speaking through all the singing, something about blood and bodies. Atticus couldn't help but only hear the reverberation from the speakers that sounded like they were playing right into his head. There was something about the little window of light framed by the mahogany doors. The cool blue sky he knew was outside, the scraping palmettos, the figure of Jesus hovering—concave and desperate—right in front of him and Mama.

He thought he didn't like the statue's eyes on him like that. Nothing simpler about it. The lower lids drooped too much, and the face was too gaunt. He looked like a tired horse. Something about him reminded Atticus of Father Abraham. It did not bring him comfort in the way he wanted it to.

Atticus tried to stay. He tried squeezing his eyes shut very tightly and he tried breathing slowly. He didn't want to stop thinking about the boars in the back yard. The image in his head was like a song he couldn't quite remember all the words to, like when Dewey would play the same tape in the car with his friends over and over until it wore out or got stuck.

That memory was comforting at least. Sometimes, if one of their girlfriends were with them, Atticus would sit on her lap in the passenger seat while they went driving, and she would almost always be the nicest to him. The girl who could speak French had first suggested that Dewey should give Atticus a beer, so he didn't like that one very much.

He had liked the one who died the best. She smoked too many cigarettes and would dance to the tapes Dewey had if she really liked the song, even if no one else was dancing. She would bounce Atticus on her knee while they were driving, even though he was starting to get too old for stuff like that, and wrap her arms around his waist with her chin on his shoulder. She would sway him in time to the music, especially if the radio started playing a ballad or something like that. She liked music that was even older than Dewey's music, which was the stuff their daddy used to listen to all the time. That was part of the reason their mama hated it so much.

Thinking of the boars helped. Thinking of his big brother's stereo and the wind pressing against his face helped.

Thinking of that dead girl made it feel like his whole chest was going to fold in on itself. It made Atticus want to cry, and he'd never cried over something that wasn't a scraped knee or a stolen toy before. This scared him a lot.

Atticus mumbled "bathroom" and pushed off the pew to hurry through the back doors before Mama noticed he was gone.

**

He stumbled into the gardens, the switch from the cool old-book air of the church to the sunbaked heat making his chest feel even worse.

His head was still stuck on the boar, the torn earth, the pink-feathered flight. The girl. The music from the radio. The swollen feeling in his throat. His ears rang. The sun hurt his eyes.

A man was standing right outside, in front of the fountain positioned against a mossy tiled wall, smoking a cigarette. He was wearing a suit and big reflective sunglasses that covered most of his face.

Something in Atticus knew to go to him.

Atticus went to him.

He lit another as the boy approached. Atticus couldn't see his eyes but knew he was staring Atticus down. That much was clear. The man spat on the ground.

"What're you doin' out here, kiddo?" He sounded drunk but he didn't smell how Dewey smelled when he was drunk. There was something hazy to him, unrecognizable. Not a kind of man who was easy to go about describing.

Atticus looked over his shoulder. A stray cat darted into the shade of a parked car. The highway buzzed like something breathing from behind the garden's tall fence and wilting wall of green. Atticus turned back to the man. The man spat on the ground again.

"What's your name?"

"Atticus," said Atticus. The man smiled. His teeth were kind of crooked.

"Atticus, okay. Very poetic." He put the cigarette back into his mouth. "You know these parts pretty well, Atticus?"

Atticus looked down at his shoes. He knew it from his mama's or Dewey's car. He wasn't allowed to walk along the highway by himself, not even to make it to the school bus on time. He knew the way back from the overpass where Dewey and his friends hung out by foot, and the way back from school, but that was just by pure luck.

"Where'd you need to go?"

"Do you remember the girl who used to live here? The one they fished out of the river, who was all over the news a couple of days back?" The man mumbled even more with the cigarette in his mouth, so it was hard to hear him.

Atticus nodded. They always passed it on the bus on his way home from school. His head was so much quieter than it had been. He wasn't sure if he was scared or not.

"Can you show me where that was?"

Atticus looked down and dragged the tip of his tennis shoe over a crack in the asphalt. "Can't go in the mangroves.

Snakes." His best friend from school got bit by a moccasin once. His whole leg turned black, or at least that's what Mama said when they went to dinner with some other parents a couple days after he'd gotten out of the hospital. Mama wouldn't let him play near any of the drainage ditches for a long time after that, but she forgot about it eventually.

"Just near it, not the—not the actual place." Something changed in his voice. Atticus wished he wasn't wearing the sunglasses so he could actually see his face. "Not the actual place."

"Okay," Atticus said. The man stretched out his hand. Atticus took it.

**

Jaime's memorial was on the overpass, right above where they spent four hours trying to get her out of the roots.

The water was darkest there. When it got too hot, a thick scum would form over top and make it all look like something solid. The river—this one was one of the only natural ones for miles—looked like the back of a big black snake from far up. From down here, it curved too much to see just how far it stretched.

The man's name was Newbury—which sounded like the name of a place and not a man, Atticus told him—and he had never been to Florida before. He was from someplace that used to be close, before the president's seawalls decided what land stayed and what went. That was way before Atticus was born, so he didn't think about that all too much. But when Newbury talked about where he came from, he realized how sad it was. That the place had to go, just like that.

Newbury spoke like each word cost him something, and he looked at the world like it was all brand new. He got scared by the cars a bunch. He spent a lot of time staring at things Atticus couldn't see.

Atticus brought him to the overpass. Atticus pointed to the memorial. Newbury let go of his hand.

Newbury stepped toward the memorial again and again. He was wearing workman's boots—scuffed and dull and too heavy for this heat.

The memorial overflowed onto the sidewalk. All the kids in her class and some more from the church left something. The news crews always filmed in front of it because all the old flowers and new ones looked good on camera. There were candles. Someone left a clay vase. He didn't know how it hadn't been smashed yet.

Newbury stood in front of the photo of the girl, his back to the highway behind them, looking at her and then the river behind it through the chain link. It was her yearbook photo, her straight black hair hanging heavy and dark over her shoulders and her eyes bright. He had his feet planted on a bouquet of marigolds.

Atticus stepped a bit closer to look at the photo with him. The wind from the passing cars pushed their clothes into their backs. Newbury put his hand on Atticus's shoulder and squeezed.

"She was pretty," Atticus said. He didn't know why, but he wanted to fill the silence. So he said the first thing that came to his mind. "She was really pretty."

The flowers looked like they didn't belong there—orange, yellow, and white against the hard cement. The smell of exhaust was thick and the unlit candles littered their feet. This was the place where they found her—or, really, right below them. Atticus knew that. This was where everything ended and began.

Newbury pushed the sunglasses onto the crown of his head. His hair was so greasy it looked wet. His hands looked older than he was, knuckles red-purple-white with dried skin. He smelled like sea salt and brine. Newbury looked back down at Atticus and squinted. Then he threw the cigarette on the ground and nodded to the photo Zip-tied to the chain link fence. "She's my daughter."

6.

NEWBURY

———

Sometimes it felt like the whole sea was coughing into his lungs.

Whole oceans, whole waves with their fish and bitter salt. It didn't feel right but it did, like his whole mouth was crusted shut and it couldn't get hotter than this, this summer. It felt like sinking your whole self in the bayou and never coming back up.

This summer, this moment, was worse than the others, worse than when he was out on the rig the summer Warren got killed. Something about the air changed, too thick. The water smelled foul and the people smelled worse. There was no ocean—the walls made sure of that—no breeze to keep the shirt from sticking to his back.

His ma told him once that he was an old soul. Too connected to the water, that's what she said. A moving spirit.

Couldn't keep the ground underneath him no matter how hard you tried. She swore it. That's what she attributed to the fleeting moments of sound and the bursts of lividity—an old soul, a water child.

Sometimes feels like whole crabs tearing at my stomach.

His ma was kind. His ma took whole nights to comb through his hair. She called him her special boy. Called him something burning. Something new. Her star child. She always smelled like clay cause of the factory she worked at where they made those big pipes to sink into the earth. *I swear I can hear them humming under my feet.*

She loved him no matter what, even when he would do nothing but stare into space for days on end or when he got so angry he put his fist through the wall or just about anything else that could have been in his way. When he was sound and when he was livid, there was always her, and her smell, and late nights driving in Warren's car.

He loved his ma like he loved the mountains that looked like faces were just trying to push through them, purple when the pale sun would rise. He loved his ma like he loved the roads he walked, or drove, or floated across whenever the bitter pill slid past his tongue.

He and Warren would spend long evenings at her kitchen table while they waited for the heat index to go down enough so they could work the neighbors' gardens for spare cash. Warren would always show her his coin tricks, and the older she got, the more excited she was when he did.

Funny how time can turn you back into a child again. Funny how things like that can work.

By the time Warren died in the drunk driving accident, she had forgotten both his name and Newbury's completely. She would ask Newbury where "that sweet boy" went and Newbury wouldn't know how to stop crying. During those few months before they were evacuated, it seemed like he never stopped crying.

The months spent on the rig never left him. He got the pill and bottle habit there because that was all any of them had to get by. And then there was Colorado, where he abandoned his mother in a nursing home and got a job because of his father's name at the local police station. He was drunk for almost every waking moment, but it kept his head quiet. His eyes dry.

In Colorado, Newbury was a detective—the good guy with a gun. He used to sit in front of a desk at all hours of the day and get scared by the sounds of police chases on the TV. He would wake up from dreams about the rig more horrifying than anything he could put into words.

That was back when he had that little apartment with the dog and the yellow curtains with red flowers all over them. Everything in that apartment belonged to the old woman who used to live there, who had died in the hallway just outside the front door. He got it for cheap because the landlord didn't want to deal with all of her old stuff and Newbury didn't mind living in someone else's home. Everything was hers, from the couch and the rugs to the lamps and the dog. He still got her mail the entire time he lived there. He kept it in a pile on the kitchen table and didn't even bother to take down the photos of someone else's family on the walls.

He really liked the dog, though—a little terrier with wiry gray fur that would jump up and bite his hands every time he left the apartment and every time he came back home. Now it was hard to remember her name, but she would knot her body in a tight curl right behind his knees each night and lick his face until he woke up at exactly 7:05 every morning. If he didn't get out of bed, she would shit in front of the television out of spite. She had a long torso and a pot belly that would make her back dip. She would jump up on the table and eat the food right off his plate with him sitting right there if he didn't react fast enough.

He didn't know what happened to her. Sometimes he missed her, sleeping in lonely hotels with too-loud air conditioning and stiff sheets. After he saw the news that one night, he lost his job the next morning, got in his car, and didn't look back.

When he was sound, *been so long seems impossible now especially now*, he could remember his daughter's name. Her birthday. He was at work when she was born. The mother's mother called him after it was all done. He remembered that much.

He got a letter in the mail months later—two photos of her. She was in a blue onesie, biting down on a stuffed bear toy. Her fingernails were very small. He put the envelope in a drawer and quickly forgot it was there. He never even wrote a single check.

When he saw the news reports coming out of Carrabelle, and they said *her* full name, he spent the rest of the night pacing in front of the drawer where he kept the envelope. He only opened it twice and could only look at the photos once. Because it couldn't have been real, to him. At least not after the initial shock.

He was in the grocery store when the news broke because maybe the world was ending, but that didn't change much about anything these days, anyway. And nothing boosted ratings more than a good old-fashioned murder mystery—*but it is so sad.* The newscaster with her fluorescent bulb teeth kept repeating. *So incredibly tragic.* She kept moving her mouth and her makeup-creased face looked too perfect to be real. *Whole life ahead of her.* Newbury thought her face was a mask, then. It wasn't real. It didn't move enough to be real.

And they used her yearbook photo, where they had prematurely photographed her in cap and gown—her smile a beaming ray of projector light. Her face was thin but kind and her slightly crooked nose was dotted with freckles. They always used the yearbook photo for the white kids. Newbury knew that much.

And the newscaster kept saying how *sad* she was, as they repeated the video taken from some bridge of a disjointed porcelain form being lifted from the roots of the mangroves. It was blurred for the comfort of the viewer, but only slightly because you could fill in the blanks easily. So there she was.

And it was *so sad*, the newscaster kept saying. But she was really saying *watch. We'll play it again. Are you still watching? Look, we will play it again. Keep watching.* He thought he was going to throw up.

And Newbury had a box of cornmeal in his hand when the story broke, he remembered. Because earlier that day he was feeling the saddest he had felt in the longest time and he wanted to make something that reminded him of his ma. So he set out toward town with a twenty-dollar-bill and a folded recipe for corn bread in his pocket.

He had walked the whole way there because something about turning the car on freaked him out. He may or may not have reached something at the bottom of two kinds of bottles immediately before deciding t1o make his mother's cornbread because he was feeling the saddest he thought he had ever felt.

The walk helped his vision go back to normal. The grocery store was saddled up right next to the interstate, so he got to watch the car headlights go by. He swore that each passing pair of high beams left trails of matriculating light behind them. The longer he stared, the more intricate the lines of interwoven yellow, white, orange, and red became, hovering like ghosts over the darkened asphalt. That night was dark in a hazy green kind of way. He didn't know else to describe it.

When he got to the grocery store, the sound of the florescent bulbs bothered him a lot more than he thought they could. The neatly lined items in their colorful packaging hurt his eyes. The squeak of his footsteps against the shining linoleum made something in his gut flinch.

When they flashed Jaime's full name on the screen, he had dropped it—the box of cornmeal—and the gritty yellow powder had gone absolutely everywhere. A woman farther down the aisle rushed to his side and asked him, "Are you okay? Are you okay? Did you know her? Are you okay?" She had her child in her shopping cart and it began to wail because its mother had run away so fast, and Newbury couldn't help but stare at the child and its little clenched fists and its bright red face.

He didn't even realize he was nodding, on his hands and knees in the spilled grit. Or that the woman was crouching too, reaching up to smooth her little hand over his back. She was saying, "I am so incredibly sorry." And her hand would move and he felt like he could feel every fiber of his shirt scratch against his skin. It took him a long time to realize that his face was wet, or that he was sobbing like a tall child in the middle of the baking goods aisle.

Newbury didn't look at TVs anymore after that. He left for Florida the next morning.

Newbury studied the photo they had attached to the overpass for a long time. This one was easier to bear. Easier than the baby photos.

She had his ma's nose. Little and crooked and slightly flat at the bridge. Her mother's eyes, most definitely. Didn't look nothing like Newbury. Her hands must have been soft in the same way Warren's were for a long time. Long time. He could tell that from just the pictures alone.

The concrete didn't feel real under his feet. The boy was looking up at him like he was trying to ask a question. He was asking a question. He was repeating himself. Her eyes in the photo bore holes into his. *Her eyes. Her smile. Her cap and gown. Never gonna walk across that stage anymore. Her cap and gown, her eyes. Her cap and gown.*

The thing was that he *remembered* being her age—being young and wanting nothing more than to throw himself into something dark and empty and never wanting to come back. There is nothing innocent about that, just the capability for some profound sadness. A writhing in the gut. He should have been there.

How old had she been? What had her voice sounded like? Did she also taste the salt? Did she also feel a fire in her throat, dream of oil lakes and dead best friends? *She is now the dead best friend to someone.* Was it in his right to mourn? *She is now the dead best friend.* What had been her mother's name?

He was finding it difficult to remember. *She is now.* The boy asked him if he was thirsty. Tired. He nodded. It was as if he were listening through water. *She is now.* Something in his stomach twisted. *She is.*

7.

ATTICUS

Sometimes it felt like Atticus was at the bottom of a great big swimming pool and everyone he'd ever met, everyone he'd ever loved, was standing up top talking down into the water. Into him.

This should have been a scary thing, but it comforted him in a way he had always known.

8 .

DEWEY

The day they found Jaime's body in the river a different kind of silence settled over the whole school.

Dewey had come in still drunk from the night before—or from the nips Rob always hid inside his football duffle bag, it was hard to tell—but even he could tell through that numb haze that something had happened.

Their homeroom teacher had been crying, and everyone was a nervous quiet. She told them there was going to be an assembly, asked them all to keep the noise down in the meantime. They took her seriously then, something none of them had ever done, but there were some sidelong glances and whispering and everyone agreed to shut up.

Jaime hadn't been in school for a couple of months at that point. She stopped showing up at the end of the previous year. All their teachers were really good at avoiding questions about her, but not too many people asked questions anyway, especially after the first few weeks.

Dewey's headache was just starting to come in at full force when they pulled everyone into the auditorium and the head of school announced in a warbling voice that Jaime had died. But that didn't keep a sinking feeling from settling in his gut. There was a murmur that rose and then quickly faded, and it looked like some kids already knew. Earlier that morning the news had showed a limp, pale body tangled in some roots. Black water reflected a sunrise and that strange white shape. It was too far away to really see anything at all so they didn't censor it or anything like that. At least not at first.

And then the teachers let them file out and that was that. The day returned to normalcy, and they sat through classes in an uneasy quiet that made something in Dewey's stomach churn and then tighten. Churn and tighten.

That night he could barely sleep.

Violet let him go to bed without sitting through dinner and let Atticus watch TV all night, even though the little shit probably had no fucking clue what was going on.

Dewey lay in bed and stared at the popcorn wall until shapes began to form in the darkness.

When he was little, his daddy would sometimes turn off all the lights in their house and it would get dark in a way Dewey had never experienced since. Growing up, there were no street lamps outside of their old house, no interstate or insomniac neighbors. Just the thick black sound of the trees around them.

His daddy would turn out all the lights, sit Dewey down in front of him, and say, "Look at my face." That dim outline of his features would twist into something that only kind of resembled a smile. And Dewey would. And the longer he looked the more his daddy's face started to disappear so Dewey would start crying. His daddy would laugh something low, turn a lamp back on, and swing Dewey around to say, "I'm right here. I'm right here." Sometimes Dewey didn't know if he could trust his own memories or not.

On his nightstand, his phone blinked to life. He groaned and rolled onto his side, wincing at the bright blue light of the screen. Rue had texted him, asking if he was still awake. Dewey rubbed a hand over his face before responding. He pushed himself out of bed, pulled on a shirt and a pair of shorts, and snuck out of the house through the window.

Rue lived four houses down. His mother was a kind woman with a violent tremor in both her hands that Dewey never asked about and Rue never mentioned. His father was in prison for a long time and only came back when Dewey had already been friends with Rue for two or three years.

Rue talked about his dad a lot, how he went to prison rather than rat out his baby brother, and then would go on some long rant about family and loyalty and the dignity that comes with it. Something about being "a real man."

Dewey would always nod through it, but he stopped paying attention to the specifics after the first time Rue gave the speech. He was pretty sure Rue knew, too, about his nodding out. They both just treated it like it was something Rue needed to get out there into the world. To reassure himself, or something.

Hell, if Dewey's father ever came back out of the blue, Dewey sure as fuck knew he would make as many excuses as possible too. Family values. Legacy, loyalty. Sure. Whatever gets you through the night.

Rue let him into the backyard through the back gate and they climbed onto the roof together using the ladder propped against his little sister's play set. They always had to be careful to avoid the window of Rue's parents' room because his mother never really slept. Rue told him once that she practically had every episode of some Housewives show memorized. All Dewey knew was that the changing light from the TV hit the curtains in a way that looked ghostly.

They had spent countless nights on that roof. This one was different. No cigarettes or beer or watered-down liquor from the cabinet above the sink. Rue had left school after assembly—just got up and left. Dewey remembered looking over at him on the bleachers and he was hiding his face in his hands. His shoulders weren't moving but he had been crying hard enough that the tears were running down his forearms.

Rob had been a dick about it said something about their relationship that Dewey was too out of it to remember. But he did remember threatening to clock Rob in the face for it.

"I'm really sorry, man," Dewey rubbed a hand over his eyes once they had settled at the edge of the roof. You could see into the other neighbors' yards from up here, and the moon sat high enough in the sky where you could just about make out the shape of a playground and a palmetto. Somewhere two or so houses over someone was still awake. He could tell by the little square of orange floating in the blue-black darkness. "Like, I'm really fuckin sorry."

Rue didn't say anything for a long time, just rubbed the back of his neck and rested his elbows on his knees. Dewey leaned back to look up at the moon.

"We never did anything," Rue said it quietly. "I know she had that reputation and I... She just didn't want to have to go home until late and so... I don't know, she needed an excuse, and she was easy to talk to. You know, how some people are just—*easy* to be around."

"Yeah, yeah I do."

"And she—I don't know. I don't know man, I—fuck. *Fuck.*"

Somewhere, a dog barked and a baby started crying. The low wail was almost drowned out by Rue's shuttering breath.

Something sat low and heavy in Dewey's chest.

"I know, I know."

**

Two weeks later, he woke up on a dusty velvet couch in Rob's basement with a broken nose and two black eyes. He was late for church—or, no, he had slept through services completely and was halfway toward getting skinned alive by Violet for not bothering to show up at all.

Either hungover or still drunk, he stumbled to his car and drove home without turning his phone back on. Rob and Annabelle were already gone, picked up by one of Mr. Fairchild's drivers to go to some kind of special viewing for the eclipse at one of "the estates." Dewey never asked what that meant because Rob always rolled his eyes in this way whenever he said it like he expected all of them to know already.

They were supposed to be back by later that afternoon to go hit a bonfire party happening on one of the beaches that Dewey agreed to go to depending on his hangover. Rue had been acting weird the night of the party, but as soon as they raided one of the medicine cabinets at around twelve, he was right back to normal. Nowhere to be found now, though. Everyone else must have cleared out beforehand.

He had to leave by squeezing through the basement window, which locked automatically with a thick clunk behind him followed by an automated beeping sound from the security system. Dewey knew he was probably being paranoid, but he didn't want to find out how Button would react to his presence without either Rob or Annabelle at his side.

Dewey had parked in Violet's spot in the garage. He grabbed a beer from the second refrigerator there and was halfway across the lawn before he noticed that his front door was wide open.

His heart leapt in his chest. His brain didn't even have time to play back how the reporters talked about the state Jaime's house was left in—windows smashed in, door ripped off its hinges, noticeable signs of attempted arson—before he was already stepping over the threshold and into the living room.

The TV was on, and he could hear the gentle hum of some newscaster's voice without focusing on what was playing.

Dewey stayed frozen in the doorway.

He wasn't exactly sure what he was looking at. The TV was louder than Violet usually let them keep it, and Atticus was sitting right in front of it, crossed-legged and leaning forward in complete, unbroken absorption. Violet's car wasn't in the garage, so Atticus either hadn't gone to church, which was unheard of, or he had—

He heard the sound of something glass being set down on tile. Dewey whipped his head toward the kitchen.

There was a man he had never seen before sitting at the counter.

He had the shotgun Violet kept under the kitchen sink across his lap, a glass of soda in one hand, his forearm propping the rest of the languid slope of his body against the counter.

It took Dewey a moment to speak. "Who the fuck are you?"

The man stayed folded in the chair and didn't say anything. Only his eyes moved when Dewey spoke. They slid to the side like he was something sedated, how gators look at you when you pass by with their heads half out of the water.

It looked like Atticus had given him the cola that the man had his hand loosely wrapped around. The heat had melted all the ice. Condensation leaked down the side of the glass and onto the tiled counter. Next to it was a napkin with one of the peaches from the tree out back on it—pink against crisp white against the salmon pink of the counter. It hadn't been touched.

"Atticus, who the fuck is that?"

Atticus didn't even pull his face away from the television. "That's Mr. Newbury. I met him at church. He's here to find who killed Jaime."

It like all the air was knocked out of him. Dewey took a step forward and didn't tear his eyes off of the man sitting at the bar.

"Does Violet know... Did she—did she invite him here?"

"He said he was thirsty and I knew we had something in the fridge," Atticus said it like it was the most obvious thing in the world, like Dewey was being stupid for not already filling in the blanks. "I gave him one of our peaches but he said he wasn't hungry."

Atticus talked about the man like he would a stray dog he found on the way back from school. Casual. Matter-of-fact. *I gave him water because his mouth was dry. I gave him food because, look, you can practically see his ribs sticking through his shirt. His pants are barely held up by that belt.*

"Answer my question, Atticus."

He didn't. Dewey opened his mouth—

"The ocean's on fire," the man spoke. Only then did Atticus turn around.

The man's voice sounded like gravel, like he hadn't had to use it in a long time. His eyes stared right through Dewey, and they were watery in a way that made him uncomfortable. Dewey looked over his shoulder. Atticus went back to watching the news, the same channel Violet always turned on in the mornings before work to watch pretty little white ladies get drunk and talk about nothing. There was an overhead film reel playing while the newscaster talked. Dewey couldn't make out much of anything besides the text scrolling along the bottom of the screen on a blathering loop. Oil leak, faulty wiring leading to combustion, unknown how many have died. The screen was filled with only thick plumes of black smoke. Dewey heard the sound of the gun being pumped.

9.

CALLIE

———

When they lost everything in Virginia, Callie spent the entire summer in the public library. It took months for all their father's resignation papers to go through, and some weird part of her wanted to stay in Virginia for as long as possible, even though she couldn't bear to spend time with her friends anymore.

She never really knew Beau as a person until that brief period of their lives. He was her older brother, sure, but he was mostly just a passing figure. A slammed door. A fight with the parents that she could hear through the walls. When she was much younger and he was starting to become a teenager, it seemed like all he ever did was sneer and scoff and sulk around the house like some annoying pet. Looking back, Callie thought that might have too much of an impression on her. It told her to steer clear, so she did.

That summer, though, he would drive her to the library and back every morning. He was older, but kinder. He got a haircut. They were the same height—according to various grandmotherly figures Callie was "tall, for a girl"—so she didn't feel the physical intimidation of him towering over her, either.

He read a lot more, and the music he listened to was less angry. Their mother had started using him as her personal therapist. Callie could see that that weighed on him more than he let on to, but he didn't lash out like he used to.

At first they rode in silence and then, a week or so in, he would play music from the old CDs they still kept under the passenger seat from back when it had been their family car. Beau liked the old music, or, more likely, the only music they still had on CDs was old. The shit their parents would listen to when they were even younger than Callie and Beau were then. She thought it was weird how he clung to a period that would never come back. To have nostalgia for an era he was never even alive for. But she didn't hate it.

One day she asked what song was playing.

She knew this was the first thing she had said to him in a long time because Beau acted noticeably shocked. He gripped the steering wheel a little tighter, and a muscle in his jaw began to twitch. "It's something by The Replacements, I'm pretty sure. I forgot what song."

It might have been the first thing she had said to him that didn't include the screaming shared over the dinner table—the usual lines of: "All of this is your fault, you motherfucker. You've ruined our fucking lives," always shouted by a different person, to a different person, every night.

"I like it," she said quietly. When he came to pick her up later that day, with the sun a swollen red-pink, low on the horizon, it was the first song he played. She closed her eyes and let it flow through her.

**

In Florida, she locked herself in her room for days after they found out her mother was having an affair with her physical trainer.

That was when Beau left for good. That was the last straw.

It was lonely. She couldn't even find it within herself to do much of anything but stare at the wilting wallpaper and the vibrant plants outside while counting her breathing. The light wasn't as different here. She didn't know why that surprised her so much, in those long and sleepy afternoons spent under her sheets. Everything else was different, so why did the light remain unchanged?

This used to be her grandmother's house. It, too, felt the same way it did since she was little.

Her grandmother was an angry woman, or at least all the memories Callie had of her were angry ones. The dining room table still had a deep groove from where she tried to spear an uncle's hand with the carving knife one unsuccessful Thanksgiving.

Callie was too young to remember anything other than her sage-green chair, or watching her mother massage her polio-twisted calves in the early morning. Her favorite lotion smelled like grapefruit. She remembered that much, the smell of grapefruit, crisp and palpable in thick swaths of air around her. Grapefruit and the gentle hum of her favorite radio show were the only memories Callie had where she was quiet—just an old woman with sad eyes and an arthritis-seized right hand.

The night she decided to finally leave her room was a week before they found Jaime's body. She snuck downstairs for a glass of water and found her mother sitting at the kitchen table in an undershirt with her head in her hands.

Callie had never seen her when she wasn't immaculately put together. Even her sleeping gowns carried an air of untouchable coolness. And yet there she was, blue jeans and a tank top with the lilac cup of her bra peeking out. Dad was gone. Callie didn't know how she knew. She just did.

Callie stopped in the doorway and stared at her mother's back for a long time. Callie thought she would turn around but she didn't. Instead, Callie poured two glasses of water, placing one in front of her mother, and retreated back upstairs.

**

Annabelle and Rob's party had been reduced to a handful of people slumped over various couches by around two in the morning. She waited for Dewey to fall asleep before crawling off the couch and sneaking out the back.

Callie walked home barefoot and threw up in the sink almost immediately after stumbling through the back door.

She looked up, her hair in sweaty and bile-clumped strings in front of her face, and found her mother seated, again, at the table.

Her mother sat at the head of the table, the only light still on being the one directly above her head. An "atrocious"—her words, not Callie's—mid-century piece with too many abstract bits sprouting off it. Though then, and maybe it was just in her drunken haze, it looked a hell of a lot like a halo.

"You okay, baby?" She was smoking a cigarette. Callie had never seen her smoke before.

"Yeah," Callie mumbled and then proceeded to throw up a second time. All rum and cherry coke and the pizza Annabelle's dad had ordered for them that Annabelle refused to eat so Callie had only picked at a piece even though she was starving because she knew how to read a room.

Her throat burned. She heaved again, squeezing her eyes tightly shut. Then there were her mother's cool hands, pulling her hair back. She made shushing sounds, and Callie felt like she was a little kid again, snotty and feverish and begging not to have to go to school in the morning.

Her mother helped get her to the bathroom and rest her cheek against the toilet's cold seat. She didn't ask any questions, none at all, which made Callie nervous, so she confessed everything—from going to the gas station and Annabelle's comment about Beau, and Dewey kissing her in front of everyone, broken nose and all, like it wasn't something to be ashamed of.

"It made me feel big," she mumbled into the toilet bowl. "It made me feel so pretty." Callie didn't realize she was crying until she rubbed an eye and her hand came away wet and streaked with thick lines of black. Her mother brushed her fingers through her hair and told her it was all going to be okay. It was all going to be okay.

Her mother kept rubbing her back until she fell asleep. She woke up the next morning with clean pajamas on, in her own bed, with a dark purple stain on her neck. She hoped she would never have to talk about that night again.

One of their last days in Virginia, Beau tried on Callie's old dinner dresses and they took photos of him in the yard using one of their mother's old cameras that didn't get sold during the move.

Their father was away signing some set of papers—either rescinding his position in office or officially selling the house. She forgot which one and it frankly didn't matter in the long run—and their mother had locked herself away in the hotel they were living out of. It was blocks away from the beach, something their father did to make their mother happy, the both of them assumed, because she was from Southern California and always got incredibly homesick when their lives turned to shit.

Beau knocked on her door that morning and told her they were going to get away, just for a little bit.

"Let's go take pictures," he said. "Something to remember this godforsaken place by."

And so they went to take pictures.

They gathered the French magazines she kept from a vacation they went on and one of her dinner dresses. They took the car to an abandoned alfalfa field a half hour outside of town. Beau rolled down all the windows and they both scream-sang along to the CD in the stereo.

They stopped at a gas station and got pocketfuls of candy and chips while artfully dodging the cashier. Beau still had his hair long and was still brave enough to wear one of their mother's pearl earrings that he put in whenever they left the house.

All this would stop inexplicably in a week's time—he would shave his head their second night in the Florida house and return from the bathroom with a different, scarier, look in his eyes—but Callie didn't know that then.

In the field, Beau posed with his chin high and shoulders caved inward until the bones in his clavicle caught the noon sun. None of the dresses zipped all the way, so they left them hanging over his body like they were those loose silks in all those old Greek statues they would see during school trips to the museum.

In her favorite photos, he was clutching the loose fabric to his chest, letting the patterns of blue and lilac gather into unimaginably complex folds. It looked like he was trying to keep sand between his fingers. It looked like the inability to let go of something fleeting, like sand between the fingers. Or rain on skin. But his head was tilted back, exposing a long, doe-colored neck. And his eyes were barely closed, like he was in the middle of a really good dream, his long lashes throwing elegant shadows down his cheeks. He was beautiful.

When she found the developed the photographs weeks later, when the silence between their family had curdled into something rancid and all-consuming, his eyes were cut into sunken black stones. His neck was cleaved in half by the shadow of his jaw. He looked nothing like he did on that day. More sinister than ecclesiastical.

She hid them in a shoe box under her bed once he had moved out without so much as a note saying where he would be or when he would come back.

Missing were the photos he took of her, trying to hide from the camera, sitting on the hood of their old car. She remembered that she had been wearing running shorts and a ratty tank top—something she would have never been caught dead in less than a year previous, when her life was populated by pearl earrings and silk blouses and rich boys with pretty smiles and prettier cars.

A smaller, weaker part of her hoped he had taken them with him, wherever he went, and that he purposefully left the ones he left for her. So she could take him where ever she was going to go. She hoped this was a peace offering and not just random coincidence.

On that summer day, he asked her if she were okay with him getting her dress dirty since the grass had already bitten into the hem of the white fabric in hues of yellow and green. She shrugged, said they weren't going to get worn anymore anyway, and took another photo.

After that, the thought of the loss of Maywich and the rest of what they had in Virginia became much easier.

Her main group of friends checked in frequently at first, and Callie tried to respond as much as she could. They stopped after a few weeks, but that didn't matter much either. They had the rest of their June to say goodbye to the town that raised them, so they took advantage of it.

She and Beau spent days on the beach and in the town, wandering even further into the countryside. She gave him books from the collection she brought back from Maywich and he carved things out of wood or soap that he slipped into her pockets when she wasn't paying attention.

They became best friends, in part out of desperation and in part as a search for forgiveness in a house where their mother never stopped endlessly crying. Their father a stone figure with eyes glued to anything that wasn't immediately around him: a phone, a television screen, a newspaper, a blurring painting of a long-lost relative nailed to the wall just over your shoulder. Anything to keep from looking at *you* in the royal sense of the word. Callie didn't have the energy to be mad at him for it.

Despite this, it might have been the happiest collection of weeks in Callie's life.

They explored the coastline, brought leftovers to stray dogs and rescued turtles off the highway tarmac. She finally got to tell someone about all the books she had read, in those previous months of silence. It was a kind of catharsis she didn't know she needed.

One afternoon, she and Beau walked along the coastline until the sands were engulfed in grass and the countryside tumbled into the water. They scaled a crumbling wall from some old fortress that had sunk into the earth. Only the wall remained, rising strong before dropping off into the ocean. Beau went first and then helped her up. They walked with their arms outspread to the end, dangling their feet over the waves.

The morning he left—she did not know it was their last morning together. She would have savored it more if she had known—they drove to their new favorite café and he gave her a book of poetry by some French woman she had never heard of before. He told her he wrote something at the back but she had to promise to read the whole thing before she read the letter. That's what he called it, a letter. He made her promise, and then they shared two cups of coffee and a cookie and talked about absolutely everything and nothing all at once. He drove her home after that, and promised he would be right back. That they needed to find another wall like that one in Virginia, even though the beach was a lot farther away now. He would be right back, he said. Right back.

When she put two and two together, that he'd never come home again, she threw the book with the photographs under a box of her old things under her bed and pretended like he had never given it to her in the first place.

The day they told everyone that they had found Jaime's body in that water, the first thing she did when she got home was pull the book back into the light. She tossed it down on her bed and watched the aubergine comforter puff up around it with its weight.

She looked at it a long time and then tucked it back under the bed.

CARRABELLE, FRANKLIN COUNTY

The state police took the girl's body before the investigation could even begin. They were the ones running the operation before they even pulled her from the water, but not a single Carrabelle officer was even present as they did so. The local officers got the news that a body had been found like everyone else did, by turning on the morning news.

The deputy, who was the only Carrabelle representative at the riverside, had a daughter who was in Jaime's English class. He remembered her from a performance they did the previous year. It was a small town, but no one said much about her. They were known as a family that kept to themselves. Nothing wrong with that.

Her face was unrecognizable from the bloat and bruising, but he was able to identify her by the tattoo on her wrist because that was what the poem she performed was all about. The deputy only remembered this because his wife had rolled her eyes and muttered "trashy" under her breath when Jaime flashed the thing at the crowd, but he didn't tell anyone that.

After that, all the local police had left was the house. It was off a little farm road, the last residency before the prison with only a handful of miles of forest separating the two.

There was a lake some of the people living off the highway would take their kids to in the summer, in the cooler months before it got too hot and the bacteria got too bad to let anyone near. Years ago, the mother of the girl once called the police department about a group of teenagers setting off fireworks from the docks. She stopped calling them about it once they asked her why the lease to the house wasn't in her name.

They sent three sets of officers to the house when they learned about the body.

Six officers quickly turned into an entire Crime Scene Investigation unit, and the other half of the force watched, like everyone else did, as they pried the girl's body loose from the knotted trees on the television screen.

The house was torched, remained so to this day as whoever signed the papers for it seemed to not exist at all. Every set of windows was shattered. It was hard to tell where the struggle started—or if there was a struggle at all—because everything inside was destroyed. Chairs smashed. Bookshelves overturned and charred. Wedding china crushed under what must have been some kind of work boot. Whoever had done this tried to start a fire in the kitchen, most likely to burn the entire house down, but something had stopped them. Or they left before they could be sure. Whatever it was, it was messy work.

Out back, a mattress, poorly hidden in the thick swaths of Florida underbrush, was soaked through with rust-brown stains. It looked to be a month or two old at least, and a family of mice had already burrowed their way through and made a home in one of the corners. That and the collection of baby toys strewn throughout the mess in the living room painted a pretty clear story.

The whole place smelled like burning plastic and overturned earth. There were clear tire marks on the front lawn that were quickly destroyed by some rookie on his first day of the job.

Everything was unsalvageable except for the girl's room, which was immaculately preserved. When one of the officers opened the door, the wind from the broken window lifted the pristine white curtains something ghostly. The popcorn walls were painted a pretty pink and the only blood was where, they assumed, the intruder smashed her head a few times with the lamp and then put it neatly back on the nightstand. The bed was still made. Even the fragile line of pots resting on her windowsill remained unbroken.

The crib in the corner of the room was robbed of its mattress, and the only significant disturbance was a box of diapers that had been overturned on the floor.

They didn't have the body so there was no way to determine the cause of death before the state made any time of confirmation, which they never did. Later, Carrabelle officers found a blood crusted plastic bag and one of the girl's belts buried down the road. When they got her out of the water, the reports of bruises on her neck were clear enough to piece together what had happened there.

The mother was nowhere to be found. The baby was untraceable, with no records at any hospital in any county saying Jaime had given birth there.

They administered an all-points bulletin for Jaime's mother and the missing baby on scene. Later, a state patrolman would tell a Carrabelle officer that they were never told nothing about *any* missing baby, and that they were only ever given the mother's information.

The state patrolman would tell the local officer this in a bar, and they would both be drunk, but the officer would remember it for a long time after.

And it nagged him to the point where he would just have to tell his wife while they were both getting ready for bed because it ate at him all night and the day following. Got the boss's coffee order wrong and everything. That's how hard he thought about it.

He came up behind his wife as she was brushing her teeth and wrapped both arms around her waist, pressing his forehead into the gentle dip of her shoulder. She spat into the sink and then brought up a hand to run through his hair, cropped close to his scalp in the same way all the other men had it. The officer's wife didn't ask what was wrong. She waited for him to come to it himself. She nodded and hummed along to whatever he said next.

"It was probably just miscommunication, darling," she said. And he nodded, kissed the shallow pool of her collar bone, and slipped away.

She would then ask him about this again, though, over breakfast. Because something about it started nagging at her, too, and she had a hard time going to sleep the night before because of it. She couldn't stop thinking about "that poor girl."

"That poor girl," she said. "And if there *was* a missing child, shouldn't all of us be doing something to make sure it is okay? A missing *baby,* for Christ's sake."

And the officer stared into his cup of coffee and just said, "I don't know. I don't know," as she pretended to clean one of the glasses in the sink.

And then the officer's wife would bring it up at her Sunday brunch, bouncing her own toddler on her knee. And the wife, who was sitting across from the chief's wife, would shake her head and furrow her brow over it. And the chief's wife would tilt her head in a certain kind of way that no one else noticed, but it was certainly a tilt of the head.

The officer would lose his job the next morning. The state patrolman would never show up at that bar to meet him again, even though they were high school buddies who had played football together and everything. And then the officer's house would be broken into. Once. Then twice. No reports would be filed about it, but the wife swore she woke up one night to a man standing over their bed. She screamed so loudly she lost her voice the next day but the man ran out before anything "really horrible" could happen. Everyone at the station, even her husband, pretended that they didn't believe her.

The officer and his wife would leave Franklin County in a week's time after.

**

Jaime's mother was found in a holding cell four towns over. It was only then that they found out she was a dancer—a piece of gossip that spread through the town like wildfire. A piece of gossip that slowly had Jaime's name disappearing from the headlines in the days that followed. Indecent. Impressive that she managed to keep that secret for so long anyway.

Jaime's mother was used to disappearing, that fading from the eye. Women like her had to be.

She'd been thrown into central bookings for involvement in a bar fight that previous night. She was still drunk when they put her in the car, mumbling how the "state got no right to take my prints like that they my damn fingers what the fuck do they think they have the right think they God or somethin think they can push me around like that fuckin' *me* they think they God or somethin those mother fuck—" and then she looked up so fast she swayed a bit. And then she asked, "Did they find Jaime yet." She slurred it as a statement, not a question. The responding officer looked over at his partner, and his partner swallowed but didn't say anything.

She threw up in the back seat as soon as they pulled onto the highway. She had been barefoot. She asked one of them for a cigarette after spitting out the rest of the bile in her mouth onto the floor of the car. She said, "My head hurts like a bitch." And then she didn't say anything else for the rest of the ride. The officer would think that the mother and Jaime had the same hair, thick and inky black. They had the same hair. And he wouldn't stop thinking about this.

At the funeral, only the mother and the two guards at the door knew the casket was empty. It didn't stop her from crying like that anyway.

10.

DEWEY

—

His earliest memory was of a blizzard. Violet knew this, but insisted they never took him nowhere with no blizzard. Swore that on her life. But Dewey knew his own damn head and so he knew his earliest memory was of a blizzard.

He remembered being young enough that Atticus was only a slight lump under Violet's shirt, and his daddy was shoving Dewey's arms through a puffer jacket, pulling a hat low over his head. The house they were in, wherever it was, had wood walls and a fireplace and a plush red rug that he wanted to rub his face all over, for some reason.

But in the memory, his daddy was shoving Dewey's arms into a puffer jacket and then tying a line of rope—the laundry line, from outside—around his waist. Tight. And Dewey didn't remember being told to do so but he knew his daddy wanted him to walk into the blizzard, to feel the whole of it, only to be pulled back to the safety of Atticus—the man—and Violet and her little lump and the fireplace and the soft red carpet.

And Dewey was so excited, for all of this, both the artificial withdrawal and then the return. The return, most of all, because he wanted to see the look on Violet's face when he came back, through that wall of white cold that was outside the cabin's open front door.

He remembered stepping outside, then, and the cold sucked all of the air out of his lungs. It only took five or so steps before the snow turned everything around him into a white shroud, and then there was only the sound of the wind.

Dewey remembered looking down at his hands, up into the white, and then back down at his gloved fingers. He supposed, really, that this was the only genuine part of the memory. That all the stuff beforehand—the laundry line around his waist for his daddy to pull him back in when the time came, the cabin and Violet inside of it—was something his mind just filled in the blanks to. He didn't even really remember the act of stepping outside.

The only thing that was certain was the act of looking down at his hands and looking back up and seeing the void of nothing. Absolutely nothing, except for the howl of the wind and that all-consuming white.

When the man, Newbury, used Violet's shotgun to get Dewey and Atticus into the car parked outside, Dewey felt like he was looking into something very similar. He felt like he was trapped in that memory of the blizzard, looking up and seeing nothing, looking down and only being able to see the movement of his hands.

"Real sorry about this," Newbury kept saying as he helped Atticus into the back seat of his car with one hand and pressed the nozzle of the Mossberg into Dewey's kidney with the other.

Dewey got in the car and Newbury slid into the passenger seat, putting the silver-mirrored aviators back over his face. His greasy hair flopped back over his forehead. He was easier to process without being able to see his eyes. For some reason it made him look more human.

All of these observations only echoed silently in Dewey's head. He did not fully process anything at all except how his fingers felt wrapped tightly around the steering wheel. Everything in him felt very cold.

Dewey watched his hands turn on the car. Watched his fingers curl and flex around the steering wheel. Once. Twice before beginning to pull out of the garage.

There was something too calm about all of it. No shouting, no demands. Just that rough yet silk-smooth voice and the pressure of the gun against his side. *Turn here*, he would say, and Dewey would turn. *Slow down.* And Dewey would ease off the gas in time to process how quickly the palmettos were whipping past them. *Turn, again. Like that. Stop crying. Who did that to your face, anyway. Why are you shaking like that. Turn here, boy. Did no one tell you how to use your blinkers. Once, I drove across the country in a car just like this, you know. Just like this one. Drove until my eyes were so tired I could barely keep 'em open, you know that feeling where everything just slows down and even the lights of the other cars get that drag to 'em. I don't wanna have to tell you again to slow down, boy. We almost there. Don't get too eager now. I'm just as excited as you are. I'm real sorry about all of this. All of this, swear it. So sorry.*

11.

ATTICUS

———

The girl who went to Father Abraham's church, the one whose daddy cried during the sermon about the dead girl, her name was Elisa. She had deep brown skin and curly hair cut close to her chin, and she wore baggy overalls roughly cut at the knees with ratty sneakers. She was mean in the way the other boys his age were mean, so Atticus didn't get made no fun of for being friends with her in the first place.

Both her mama and her daddy were nice enough people who worked on one of those corporate farms north of Tallahassee, so she lived most of the time with her grandma, who had soft hands and a bald head like an egg. She said she could talk to ghosts when she sang. Atticus liked her singing voice but didn't believe in nothing haunted. Their house felt too kind for anything like that.

Elisa told him he couldn't say that he didn't believe in God because her grandma only liked her friends who went to church. Atticus never told Elisa if he did or didn't believe in God, but he took her instructions well, even said Grace one time at dinner. They had a scratchy blue and white carpet under their dining room table that hurt his feet even through his socks, but he didn't mention it because the food was good enough to make it worth it, and her grandma really did have a pretty singing voice.

Elisa's parents worked as cattle farmers, and once they came back for Christmas with a calf that was going to be slaughtered because it was born "hot" and tied it in their backyard. Elisa told him how she and her mama would wake up every few hours to keep her fed. How the food they gave the calf's mama caused little white dots to form in the eyes of her baby. Just like little stars. Elisa told him how the calf's insides were all scorched and they knew she wasn't gonna live long. But at around two weeks into keeping her, Elisa could play around with her like she would a dog, wrestling and jumping around and everything.

"That thing would hop around and butt at the air and swing its big head around just like a puppy would," she told him. They were in her grandma's yard the day before Atticus would meet Newbury in the church gardens. The unkempt grass threw off flurries of lawn moths with each movement they made.

She was playing with one of the uprooted shoots of the overgrown St. Augustine grass. Atticus always knew when her parents finally came back home for a visit because the lawn would be neatly trimmed by the next morning. He could tell it had been weeks because the grass tickled at their elbows when they sat down.

Elisa's grandma liked to keep things in a state of decay. She never turned on the air conditioning, even though, according to Elisa at least, her parents spent a whole lot of time saving up to get one just to keep her comfortable. During the day, her grandma would fling open all the windows and doors and let just about everything come crawling in. Elisa said she'd woken up to an iguana in her bed more than once.

Atticus liked their house because it always gave him the same feeling he got when he looked out the kitchen window with his mama and saw the evidence that the pack of boars had passed through again. She always seemed a little extra happy on those mornings, at least. His mama would never let anything like that in her own house, but a little part of her was drawn to the wild in the same way that had taken over Elisa's grandma because she never did nothing to stop them, and she always let things stay a little overgrown so they would pass through and feel safe. Maybe Atticus had the tendency to read a little too deeply into things, or maybe that was just the way he liked to see things for now.

"When it died, papa fished three of its teeth out of its mouth and gave them to me for safe keeping," Elisa scoffed at that, snapping the piece of grass in two. "Whatever that means." She kept playing with the grass. Her face screwed up in a way that looked like she wanted to say something but didn't know how to say it. Atticus kept looking at her and waited until she could put into words whatever it was she wanted to say. "Grandma said something to me last night and I don't know what she meant by it."

"What did she say?" Atticus had to screw up his face some too, but that was just because the sun was getting in his eyes.

"She keeps thinking I'm my mama," Elisa was looking at her feet. Her grandma had plaited her hair into two tight braids that morning, her black-brown curls pulled taught except for the two nubs at the base of her neck where the hair stuck out from behind the elastics like little cotton balls. Elisa had made a face when Atticus first saw her but didn't mention anything about the change of hairstyle. He didn't know her ears were pierced until then. "Which is like, fine, I guess. But she keeps saying that she's worried for my daddy, which doesn't make sense anyway because my parents didn't know each other yet when they were my age, but I guess she's confused because she's old."

Atticus just nodded because he wasn't sure what to say at all.

"This morning she put her hand on the back of my neck and told me she was worried about papa working with some guy named Fairchild and that God was going to be unhappy with me if I kept letting him do business. And then she said—" Elisa paused and looked up at the sky like she was trying to remember the exact words. She recited them like she recited the slogans they made them memorize in school, eyes upturned, each word coming a little slow so she knew she was getting it exactly right. "'What is Elisa going to do when she finds out that the only reason she has a roof over her head is because her papa spoon feeds drugs to people who are just trying to get better?'"

There was a quiet that felt like it lasted a long time. Elisa went back to picking at her pieces of grass.

"Can I see the teeth?" Asked Atticus. "Of the cow?" He had his legs drawn into his chest so he could rest his head on his knees.

"Yeah." Something in her voice sounded like she was thankful he didn't ask about anything she had just said. Elisa stood up and stuck out her hand. They were at that point where all the girls were starting to get a lot taller than all the boys. Atticus took her hand and they walked back into the house like that together.

During the day, her Grandma only let natural light into the house. It got noticeable once you strayed from the living room, with its big sliding glass doors that opened into the backyard, and ventured into the kitchen with the one window placed above the sink.

Her grandma said it was better on her eyes that way. There was a reason she could still read in the dark "at this age." They never knew what age she actually was. Elisa said she had asked her mama when she was younger and she had just laughed and said, "Now don't you worry about that."

Elisa told Atticus that she didn't want to know now because she loved her grandma and would miss her a lot when she was gone. Atticus understood something about this completely.

They walked into her room and Elisa had to balance on her dresser to reach the top shelf. She pulled out a jewelry box and set it back down on the floor, it had her last name carved on the top in looping script. Elisa hesitated for a moment, drumming her fingers once over the name—the soft pad of her finger drifting over the P, É, R, E and then tracing the Z with a flourish—before unhooking the latch and opening the box.

"My Granddad made this box for my papa. It used to carry all of his baby stuff, his first shoes and everything," she was looking inside and her mouth screwed up and drew to the side. It looked like she was thinking about something real hard. "Now we share it, I guess."

Atticus got on his hands and knees to look into the box. Every object was wrapped in white linen and nestled in gentle little rows. Some of the cloth looked older than the others, more yellowed and frayed with time and heat. Atticus thought it looked like a chest of sleeping ghosts.

ABBOT, PISCATAQUIS COUNTY

———

Shug hid his head in his hands.

He was crying, one eye swelled so severely the tears just wet the purple tissue that had become the skin stretched across his cheekbones. The blood of his split lip mixed with the saliva slowly dripping down his chin. He wept silently, shoulders shrinking into himself to conceal the mess of his face, and he pulled his windbreaker closely around him. The adrenaline made it hard to focus on any one thought, and his hands wouldn't stop shaking and it felt like the echoes of the police sirens were boring holes straight into his head.

James, who was driving the car, had bruised knuckles and a clenched jaw. He squeezed the steering wheel tightly as a muscle just below his earlobe twitched with the ferocity at which he ground his teeth. The gun on his lap did not catch any form of light, its metal a dark void against the leg of his pants.

There was only the sound of the two of them breathing for a while.

Then: "Do you remember the way she ran toward the crib?" Shug spoke into his hands once they were on the highway and the sounds of the sirens had long since faded away. His heart was still pounding from the run to the car, backpack and pockets heavy from what they managed to loot before the cops were called.

"Shut the fuck up." James spat out almost immediately, dragging a shaking hand through greying hair. "Just shut the fuck up."

"She went straight for the crib when we came bursting in there. As soon as you kicked down that door she was up and running. How could we have known? He didn't tell us fucking nothing. There's no way he could have expected us to— She didn't even scream she—"

"Quit being such a fucking faggot and put that fucking gun away."

"Ja—"

"PUT IT AWAY."

Shug jumped, hands fumbling with the gun in the driver's lap.

Behind them there was a backpack stuffed with valuables and a child's car seat. Shug held a gold watch that he had stolen from the inn in his left hand, the clock's face leaving a concentric circle pressed into the skin of his palm.

He put the watch and the gun in the glove box, shoving it away with hands that wouldn't stop shaking.

"Turn the radio on," James ordered. The tattoo on his neck, a scarab, its heavy green-black lines stretched over his jugular, rippled whenever he talked angry. Shug reached out a shaking hand, pressing an index finger against the console.

More pines. More blacktop and clouded skies. He hated Maine. He hated this sorry town with its endless backroads and highways and sleepy inns with kind ladies who didn't know shit about keeping themselves safe. *Didn't know shit, didn't see a single thing coming. Fuck. Fuck.*

Because the thing was, he looked at the innkeeper and saw that girl. The child's mother, with the pretty hair and prettier face before they got to her. Shug had backed up plenty of James's hits before but never like *that*. And Shug had robbed plenty of people, but something about stealing from the innkeeper like they did, even though she had called the cops on them. After all her kind looks at Shug and the baby and her asking of, "Is everything alright? Are you okay?" all that stuff he was keeping in just—

Shug leaned his head against the window and pressed his knees into his chest, the palm with the mark of the watch against his chest. "I want to go home."

James cursed under his breath before expelling a lungful of air in a cruel laugh. "You can't pull that shit on me now."

"We can't do this. We aren't made for this—"

"Too late," James gritted out. "Too late for you to be saying shit like that, Shug. You can't pull that kind of shit now.. You just can't." Silence, for a long time. The fog was so oppressive it coated the road before them in milky white comfort. A car passed, so did a river, a wall of rocks where some group of workers cut the highway through an immovable mountain. Chipped away soil and limestone so one day these two could pass through this disintegrated monument of nature. "It passed. It happened. We did that and now it is over," James's voice came a bit more softly then. "It was weeks ago. You need to get the fuck over it. I can't have you breaking down after every time we do something like it again."

Shug was quiet before speaking quietly into his lap. "We don't belong here."

In his head, he continued his litany with the same desperation. *With the honeysuckles, the ones that would grow over the porches. The moths we'd catch in our rooms and cup in our hands and release out the windows. We belong in front of that TV our families shared, where your mama and mine would make dinner together while we watched the news because that was the only channel we could get. Where everything smelled like lavender detergent and where your daddy would take the place of mine and teach the both of us how to hunt. We belong with the cicadas, and that summer you dropped out but still picked me up from school every day.* He couldn't manage that, though. He couldn't put those memories into words. It was something beyond the both of them. "We belong in that place before all of this, James. Home. We belong there." James flinched at his name, or maybe it was the desperation in his partner's voice.

The silence was longer this time, not heavy but just a different type of still. The car burst through the trees as the road wound into mountainous hills. Small houses dotted the skyline. There were cows and horses, a ramshackle cabin swallowed in the gray-blue light of the clouds. A stray dog. In the distance, an abandoned mine pressed against the mountain's crested face.

James took a deep breath. "The restaurant, you mean."

"What?"

"The restaurant, the one you wanted to start after school ended." James adjusted his grip on the steering wheel, clearing his throat uncomfortably. "Back when I had that job with the mechanic, remember? We were gonna rent out that little apartment above it and you were gonna take it over once Leo bit the dust. The two-bedroom, with the sink that didn't work and the windows that wouldn't open—you said we wouldn't have to worry about that because I would be there to fix it up. Like you said, before all this." The sick feeling in Shug's stomach knotted and expanded. "I think you're right." The tattoo on James's neck flexed when he swallowed. "You don't belong here."

In the back seat, the baby blinked her heavy eyes open and began to squall.

Shug bit his knuckles and hid his wet face between his legs.

12.

CALLIE

———

Annabelle Fairchild invited Callie to the Fairchild house for a sleepover the second week of school. They were paired together for a biology lab and Callie had complimented Annabelle on her skirt and Annabelle had said, "Thanks it's from—" and then said the name of some boutique that Callie didn't know at all but she nodded and smiled anyway.

Annabelle invited Callie to come to the mall with her and another girl by the end of the period. The other girl was loud and sweet but Callie almost immediately forgot her name. Annabelle carted them around to all of her favorite stores and they picked through clothes while Annabelle told Callie everything she needed to know about everyone. Her words, not Callie's.

In the middle of a story about someone giving someone else head in the fourth-floor stairway Callie quickly put together that Annabelle was confident only in her cruelty to others.

Callie kept that observation to herself.

When Callie slept over the first time, they stayed up too late watching movies and talking in Annabelle's room. They made each other laugh in that stomach-pinching, out of breath kind of way, and it was the first time in a long time Callie was able to do that without thinking about anything going on at home. It was really nice.

At one point, maybe around two or three in the morning, Annabelle hopped off her bed and got a bottle of nail polish from her dresser drawer. It was a denim blue color that Callie thought was absolutely garish, but she didn't say anything and just continued to pick at the pink terrycloth stuffed frog Annabelle had on her bed.

"I wanted to get a snack from the kitchen," Annabelle said without prompt while blowing on her fingers. She examined them carefully, with a cautious thumb and index finger plucking away the apparent dog hair.

Callie wasn't sure how to respond so she just said "oh." It made her feel a little dumb after, but Annabelle spoke again before she could begin to feel too embarrassed about it.

"The other day Mr. Cohen called me Jaime," Annabelle said as she began to paint on the base coat. She sat on her white shag rug with one tan leg tucked underneath her and the other thigh pressing against her chest so she could rest her chin on her knee cap.

"Huh?" Callie shifted on the bed, pulling the frog into her lap. She wasn't sure why she did that.

"Mr. Cohen called me Jaime, like, twice during class." Annabelle cursed under her breath when she realized she had already creased her right pinky nail on her palm when she started painting her left hand. She got up and opened the same drawer, fishing out a bottle of polish remover before continuing. "It was so weird. Everyone noticed it expect for him."

"That's super weird."

"I told Rob about it and he laughed really hard. Asshole. He told me I was making it up." Annabelle didn't sit back down. She was looking in the mirror over her dresser. Callie looked at her looking at herself and then looked at Annabelle's reflection with her. "I get it because like, similar hair and everything. And apparently she was his like, teacher's pet or whatever. But do you think we look alike? Like, really?"

Callie didn't know how to answer that question so she just shrugged instead.

Annabelle made a face in the mirror and then let her face relax. "I think she's really pretty, you know." The police hadn't found Jaime's body at that point. This was before everything changed. Though from the reports, her body was somewhere in the river's current by that point. "Especially when she lost all that weight before she went MIA or whatever." Jaime had always been thin—Callie heard the other girls talking about it a lot—so she wasn't sure what Annabelle meant by that.

"I've come home early from volley ball practice a couple of times and she was here with Rob for some reason, and she was always really nice to me. You know, junior girls aren't usually nice like that. They don't have to be to us at all at least. There's no obligation there, but she was super sweet," Annabelle looked down at her hand wrapped loosely around the neck of the nail polish remover bottle and then shrugged. "I heard she's a slut though."

Annabelle went back to painting her nails on the floor and told Callie that Rob was thinking of throwing a party the night before the eclipse. Soon after, the local police would be pulling Jaime's body from the water. Annabelle would tell Callie that Callie had made up that conversation and they would never talk about it again, even though for some reason Callie would really want to know why a girl like Jaime was spending any one-on-one time with a guy like Rob. It would eat at her a bit, but she would quickly begin to forget it too. Besides, whatever Annabelle said was what goes. Callie sussed that one out pretty quickly.

**

"It's good that you're making friends," her mother told her through the steam rising from the pot of boiling water. It was three days before Beau disappeared. He'd stopped coming to dinner at that point and stayed locked in his room for days at a time. "That Annabelle girl seems very nice."

Callie shrugged and kept her eyes glued on the onion she was chopping. "Yeah, yeah totally." She kept her hair in a low ponytail—this was before she realized how fat it made her face look—but had to keep pushing her fly-aways back with her inner forearm. "Her dad is super nice. He made us dinner when we came over and asked me a lot about—" she was about to say Virginia but she caught herself just in time, "—how the new school and everything was. Super considerate."

Her mother was silent. Callie glanced up hesitantly. She looked older in this light—more tired, her white boatneck shirt revealing the ridged peaks of her collarbones. "That was very nice of him to do," was all she said.

The silence that followed was crushing.

"Listen, I—I know he was like, an old work friend of Dad's or whatever," Callie went back to chopping. Garlic, now. Suddenly it was the most interesting thing in the world. "But I swear he didn't ask about any of that. Nothing at all. He doesn't even do politics anymore. He owns a string of those rehab clinics over in Tallahassee. And even if he was still into the whole election stuff I wouldn't have—"

"Carol Anne," her mother's voice got that sharp kind of quality to it. The treatment she only ever used to give to Beau nowadays. "I don't care about what was or wasn't said. Alright? Your father ruined his own career—hook, line, and sinker. We came to Florida to start over. No more elections, no more press. It will just be us as a family now. A clean start. That's that."

That was the dinner where her father accused her mother of having an affair. Slammed the pieces of her lover's jewelry down on the table and shouted a bunch of words that didn't make a whole lot of sense to Callie but probably still made sense to him with how angry he was.

And her mother did nothing but look down at her hands loosely clasped on the table, so that was how they all knew it was true. And once her father had gotten done with all his yelling, he kind of hesitated for a moment, and his entire face fell in a way Callie had never seen a face fall on a grown man before. He quietly sat back down in his chair and they stayed like that for a long time before Callie broke the stillness by getting up from her seat and walking back upstairs to her room. And that's where she stayed for a long time.

Beau disappeared three days later.

And that was that—hook, line, and sinker.

**

Once, back in Virginia, Callie walked downstairs and saw her parents embracing in the living room. Her mother was still holding the newspaper limply in one of her hands, like she wasn't expecting it to happen but it did. They were embracing in the living room and Callie was pretty sure her father was weeping in some kind of weird way, but they were so incredibly still at the same time—his face pressed into her neck, his shoulder hunched, her arms cupping his back with that newspaper being squeezed between her palm and thumb and index finger. Her chin was against his shoulder and, in turn, her eyes were open and looking at something far outside of the window behind him. Just like that. Like statues.

**

Dewey had tasted like blood.

She woke up from the party the next morning with his metallic taste still in her mouth—either it was that or the vomit.

She would never know that she had taken his virginity. The memory of green-velvet couch he pressed her into that left dust clinging to the sweaty arch of her bare spine left her feeling unclean for a long time after.

She remembered texting Annabelle as s1he walked home that she was just feeling really sick and so she went upstairs to lie down but she forgot Annabelle's dad was still up there, so she just walked home instead. Annabelle would be skeptical at first but she would buy it eventually because Callie knew she would never be brave enough to ask Rob why Callie and Dewey were "just talking" for so long anyway. Also, possibly, Annabelle wouldn't be able to fathom a guy like Dewey with a girl like Callie. Callie was having a hard time putting all the pieces together herself anyway.

That morning, Callie blearily rolled over and picked up her phone from the nightstand. Eight calls from an unknown number. It was noon, and all her joints ached and her stomach revolted against her if she tried to sit up too fast.

Her mother had dressed her in pajamas and helped her into bed, cleaning up the most of the vomit from her face, giving up on her hair and just knotting it in a tight bun at the nape of Callie's neck. Callie remembered some of this, the gentle cooing that came with it as she profusely apologized through her heaving.

As soon as she got out of her bed, she stripped it to the mattress and shoved her sheets into the hamper. This had become a ritual, something she had always done after the other boys she had slept with. Something about doing that made her feel like she was starting over. Hot shower, scrub brush, forget like it ever happened once everything else was clean. What had Annabelle said that one time? "Suddenly I'm a virgin again?" Yeah, that. Simple stuff.

Callie stood with her back hunched under the shower for a long time. She scrubbed every inch of her scalp and tried to ignore how much her neck hurt or how her stomach lurched every time she moved her eyes too fast in one direction or the other.

When she got out there were two more missed calls. She walked downstairs and began to make herself eggs and a piece of toast. The number called her again, and this time she picked up, pressing it to the side of her face with her shoulder as she plucked the piece of bread from the toaster, burning the pad of her thumb and forefinger in the process.

"Hello?" She spoke hesitantly after picking up to hear nothing but what sounded like distant breathing.

"Callie?"

Something in her stomach dropped. She hesitated for a moment.

"Dewey?"

"Yeah, uh, I'm real sorry about this. Listen um. I am kind of in a tight spot right now and I—"

"What do you mean? How did you get my number?"

"You—you gave it to me last night I am pretty sure but—okay, listen, listen I know you don't go to church or nothing, is there any chance you're still at Rob's right now? It's urgent."

"Dewey what the hell are you on about? What do you mean am I at… What is going on?"

"Listen I just—I know Annabelle gave you an extra set of keys for when they were going back to New York and I—listen I just need to get into their house real quick, okay? It's kind of urgent."

"I can't even begin to—Dewey are you fucking with me right now? Are you on something or some shit?" She caught sight of the hickey, again, in the mirror and something twisted in her stomach again. Not in a good way, and it definitely wasn't the hangover. She paused, and in that moment something changed. Dewey let out a breath in a certain way and she finally recognized his absolute panic. "Okay. Okay—" She pushed her wet hair back and away from her forehead. "Okay let me just get dressed, I guess. I'll be right over."

13.

ATTICUS

———

When Newbury forced Dewey out of the car with Mama's gun, Atticus didn't get scared in the way he saw Dewey get scared.

Elisa's grandma told him that he knew how to read a soul. He didn't know what that meant at all but he knew Newbury reminded him of Father Abraham in some kind of way so he knew he could trust him. That was fact enough.

"Get me in the house," Newbury said. He had a way of repeating himself but not in a way that sounded manic at all. Reassuring, kind of. Graveled and bubbling but also liquid smooth, like smoke. "Just get me in the house and I can put this stupid thing away and we can all be over this, yeah? We can all go home safe and sound."

"Okay," Atticus didn't like the sound of Dewey's voice, though. It was hard to see anything from the back seat but it sounded like he was trying not to throw up. "Okay, listen man. Listen I—Rob isn't answering his phone, okay? So I called my—my friend over. She's just a kid, man. She's just a kid so don't go swinging that thing around her okay let's just—I agreed to help you, alright? She said she was gonna be right over so just, let's just keep our heads on straight yeah?"

"Yeah," Newbury didn't remove the gun from Dewey's side. It stretched over the console between them. All Atticus could see was Newbury's hands—one wrapped around the grip, one around the forend—and the backs of their shoulders. Newbury was still wearing his dress shirt. He had left the jacket and the tie back at the house and had pushed the sleeves up to his elbows. The gun looked like it didn't reflect any light at all. It was a big, dumb, black shape against the light coming in through the windshield.

They were pulled into the driveway of a big, big house. It looked like one of the ones Violet would always whistle real low at whenever they would have to drive through the nice suburbs to get to Elisa's house two towns over. It had the really tall hedges around it and everything though it looked like no one had watered them in a long time.

It took them kind of long to get there because Dewey got really bad at remembering where Rob lived all of a sudden, but as soon as they got into the car Atticus looked down at his sneakers and saw one of his model roughneck soldier figurines just under the passenger seat. It must have fallen out of his pocket. He usually brought it with him to church so he had something to do during the boring parts. He smiled to himself and picked it up, fiddling with his arms a bit before holding it loosely in his lap.

He got it for Christmas from one of the boys at school. Elisa told him that all the farm workers' kids got them too, so he shouldn't feel so special. She then said her daddy told her it was just a way that the government tried to get kids to like them more, and that her daddy said it was bullshit and just made kids think that being mean to your workers was an okay thing to do. Then she had to explain to him what the word "propaganda" meant, but Atticus didn't really care all that much and it sounded like Elisa didn't really know what it meant either. He liked the toy because the roughneck had big muscles and Atticus wanted to have big muscles like that one day too.

Atticus leaned his head against the car window to peer outside. He could see a part of the backyard through the wrought-iron gates, littered with beer cans and broken glass that caught the afternoon sun. A floatie of a pink flamingo drifted lazily around the curve of the pool visible through the bars and then out of sight. He started fiddling with his toy more.

"She's walking down the block. I can see her just over there." Dewey's voice.

"So then get out."

"What?"

"Get out of the car. Tell her what is going on and that I have your mother's gun and your poor little baby brother is in the back seat. Tell her to give her phone to me and we will all get along just fine."

Atticus glanced up again when he heard the door slam and watched through the window as Dewey walked toward the girl with frizzy hair and flip-flops. She was kind of pretty, but her eyes were a little far apart and she walked like she didn't want anyone to look at her.

Dewey grabbed her by the arm, hard, and whispered something into her ear. Atticus and Newbury watched her face drop, her eyes go wide and her mouth part. She looked at the car, and then back at Dewey, who was still talking to her, and then back at the car.

Newbury made a sound low in his throat and then got out of the car too. He moved like a cat would, slowly but assured. He motioned for Atticus to get out of the car as well.

Atticus left the toy on his seat and took Newbury's hand. It was warm and dry. He smelled like the ocean when it was about to storm.

When they walked toward Dewey and the girl, the girl was fishing a spare set of keys out of her pocket with steady hands. She started speaking as Newbury approached.

"Listen, I don't want any trouble at all, alright?" Atticus had to squint to look up at her. The sun was getting bright. He wondered how she felt looking up at Newbury and only seeing her own face in his aviators. She looked scared, but her hands weren't shaking. She had her phone between her thumb and her index finger, holding it out for Newbury to take. He did.

"Alright," Newbury took the phone, dropped it on the ground, and crushed it with the heel of his work boot. Atticus forgot he was even wearing them. They were smeared with some kind of tar. Newbury pushed his sunglasses to the top of his head and went back to holding Atticus's hand in one hand and the grip of the gun loosely in the other. He nodded toward the house. "You mind?"

The girl, her lips pressed thinly together, looked at Newbury for a long time. Then she glanced down at Atticus, her now-broken phone, and then back up at Newbury. She started to walk toward the house. The three of them followed.

As soon as they stepped into the entranceway, a big black dog came running at them, barking. Newbury shot it.

The girl screamed. Dewey shouted a curse.

The shot didn't kill the dog but it wasn't like it could get back up either. It just made sound.

Newbury stepped over it. So did Atticus, but it was more of a hop. Inside the house was even prettier than the outside, disregarding the dying dog. Atticus really liked the floors, the shiny kind of hard wood that he would see in TV shows and movies that looked like it could stretch on endlessly.

They had a big staircase and even bigger windows. The ceilings were so high the whole place felt pretty empty for some reason. There was practically nothing on any of the walls, not a single family photo or painting. The living room had long, stained, white couches. The coffee table and kitchen counters were littered with more cans, bottles, and disposable cups.

Atticus turned to look over his shoulder, back at Dewey and the girl. She was crying, holding onto the doorframe and looking at the dog, and Dewey had his hand wrapped tightly around her forearm, trying to pull her into the house. He kept saying something like: "Please, Callie. He has my brother. Please I promise he won't hurt us but he has my brother."

So her name was Callie. Atticus thought that was a pretty name. Atticus looked up at Newbury and saw he was moving his jaw from side to side kind of slowly, but with a lot of force, like he was thinking real hard. It made a muscle just above the corner of his jaw twitch repeatedly. His pupils were really big, and it made it look like he was seeing everything and nothing at once.

The living room opened up into the backyard with a great big set of sliding doors making what was inside and what was outside nearly incomprehensible. Atticus didn't think he'd ever been in a house this nice before.

The girl disabled the security alarm by punching in some numbers on the door. She turned around. She was still crying. "Listen I don't know what you want but—"

"He killed Jaime."

Atticus felt all the breath leave the room. He looked away from what was behind the girl and up at Newbury, too. Dewey looked like a fish on land. Atticus thought that was embarrassing, so he made sure he didn't look at his brother at all.

For a moment there was only the sound of the dog's whining. It made it kind of hard to think.

The girl spoke first. "What?"

"The owner of this house. William Fairchild. He killed Jaime."

That was Dewey's rich friend's last name. Atticus remembered that. He didn't look to Dewey for his reaction in case it was embarrassing again. Atticus had known the name had sounded familiar when Elisa told that story about her grandma.

Callie, again, "What?"

"Just…" Newbury took a deep breath. Callie looked a little more afraid then, if possible. Newbury used the gun to point to the corner of the room. "Stay right there, alright? The both of you go sit down and stay right there and nothing happens. Face the wall. Whatever you hear, you didn't hear it. Atticus is coming with me."

And so Atticus went with him, up the stairs and down the long hallway of doors. He remembered that when Mr. Fairchild's wife died, they moved into a much smaller house. Rob always complained about it whenever Dewey had his friends over, even though he wasn't supposed to. Atticus wanted to think that he understood a little bit of it at least, about not wanting all the empty space, even though there was plenty of that in this house, too.

Newbury didn't know anything about that, though, so maybe that's why it seemed like he didn't care at all how much of their stuff he ruined—kicking in every door they passed like that, knocking down what little photos there were on the walls of the hallway, cracking hinges with the weight of his boots.

It looked like he found what he wanted when he busted into a door that led into what looked like some kind of an office. Atticus followed after Newbury and stood at the threshold while Newbury stood in the center of the room, looking a bit lost, a bit like the dog that finally caught the squirrel and didn't know what to do next. He went to the desk. It was big and made of heavy dark wood and took up too much space, like it thought it was bigger than the room itself. Newbury flung open every drawer in the room and emptied the contents onto the floor.

"You know how to read, kid?"

"Yes," Atticus crossed his arms in front of his chest. Elisa helped him because she was a year older and had an easier time with spelling. A little part of him was mad that Newbury thought he couldn't.

"Look for the papers that have the words 'East Repairs Company' and 'invoice' at the top. In big letters. And just below it the word 'Client 16.'" Newbury emptied all the boxes on the shelves and all the folders in the drawers, and then he got on the ground and started looking through them all. Atticus too. He wasn't sure how long it took them to gather the little pile of twelve or so pages but when they did, and Newbury sat back against the desk with all of them in his lap. He reached into his pocket and took out a phone, stacking it on top of the papers. It had a pink case and a cracked screen. Newbury put the pile on the floor in front of him and rubbed his hands up and down his thighs once, rocking a bit before stilling completely.

He said, "There she is," and it was the saddest Atticus thought he'd ever heard another person sound.

1 4.

NEWBURY

When he was young, Warren took him by the arm and dragged him to a photography show at the public museum. It was filled with artifacts from a different age, a time where people like *them* cared about people like Warren and him. One of their teachers at school told them about it, and Newbury didn't know how Warren got enough for the bus fare but trailed after him regardless. Their teacher told the whole class that they had to go, that this was the last leg of the tour before everything was gonna start getting locked up for a long time. "For safe keeping," their teacher said. This was two years after the evacuation drills had started, and all of the museums along the coast started to get increasingly empty.

Everything was in black and white, so Newbury thought it would be boring, but as Warren dragged him through photographs of slaughterhouse workers and street performers, freak shows and men dressed as women, he thought he could stay there forever.

They waited in a long line to get in for free, and the security guards would follow the two of them with their eyes in every room they weaved their way through. They spent a long time looking at the photos from some pro-war protest—neither of them knew what war—but there was some quality to it, some kind of insistence on the people's faces. Warren whispered that he thought it was probably a bad one. That those people were wrong. Newbury didn't really understand how he and Warren knew, they just did.

Warren took him by the arm and they looked at a silver-print rendering of a gravestone. It read: *Killer.* Warren had leaned into Newbury and whispered into his ear that if you did the math, the kid was only twelve years old. Older than them but just close enough for some sort of kinship, some sort of correlation, to be formed, just enough.

They both knew what it was to be erased to a nickname on a grave, to be reduced to just a collection of letters and numbers. Warren had smiled real wide and asked Newbury to put that on his headstone if he made it to the ground first.

"Gotta promise," Warren had said, and his breath had ruffled the hair on the side of Newbury's head. Two lonely kids, holding hands in front of a picture older than any lineage they could trace. Two lonely kids, leaning into each other like two tired and hungry beasts.

So Newbury said, "I will," and squeezed Warren's hand, refusing to look away from the photo. *Killer.* "I will."

**

The night before he met Atticus and got the gun, he had a dream about the supermarket. Again.

The violently colored labels of the produce twitched and withered on their shelves. The woman who held him was at the end of the aisle. She did not have a face but this did not give him fear. If she'd had one, he knew it would have been kind. He needed to know where her baby went. Newbury stepped forward and she was gone.

He woke up to a knocking on the door.

Newbury pushed himself up to a sitting position and rubbed a hand over his face. He only kept on the television, sound off, and the bedside lamp. The motel's wallpaper was beige with thick green and red stripes. He went to the door.

He bent slightly to look through the peephole and saw a woman's face—not the woman from the supermarket, the one who was kind to him—but rather Jaime's mother. Bell.

He remembered her name now because her mother had written her full name and a phone number down on the back of Jaime's baby photos. Newbury only had the courage to open the envelope once he got to Florida. The phone number was disconnected. He spent three days making calls before he finally remembered the name of the club they met in—could have sworn he was in love, back then, nearly stuck around, swore he did—and worked backward from there.

He couldn't look at the news anymore, and the high school wouldn't give him nothing. Too many people trying to poke their nose in the town's business.

Bell looked tired and hung over, her bloated stomach stretching the American flag tank top she wore and bony legs exposed by a pair of cut off shorts. Her shins were covered in bug bites. He couldn't honestly remember what she looked like back then, but he thought the eyebrow piercing might be new. He thought he remembered the stars that started behind her ear and curved down her shoulders, but he could be wrong.

"She never looked nothing like you," was the first thing she said after she sat down on the ugly flower-printed armchair next to the radiator. She tapped out a cigarette from the pack in her back pocket. Bell sat like a man would, with her elbows on her knees and her face all screwed up like she was thinking about what she wanted to say next really hard. "Wouldn't even know she was your child if it weren't for that nose of hers. That was the only thing that made me sure."

Newbury didn't know what to say so he didn't say anything.

She turned her head over her shoulder and narrowed her eyes at the television. Newbury glanced over too. The reporter's mouth was moving but no sound came out. The scrolling line of text at the bottom said something about the eclipse. There was a jolting cut to a commercial where a man with teeth too big for her mouth smiled listlessly up at the camera. Newbury had to look back down at the floor to keep from feeling sick.

Bell let out a quiet but cruel kind of laugh. "It feels like the end of the fucking world. This whole everything, I feel like it's all about to come crashing the fuck down."

They looked at each other. Newbury said, "I know," and felt like a weight was lifted off of his chest. She nodded to herself, closed her eyes, took a deep breath, and fished a phone out of her back pocket. She gave him the phone.

"It's all there." She got up. Newbury stayed on the edge of the bed with the phone cupped between his hands. He followed her with only his eyes. "He's got those *old,* old money connections. She was an idiot for thinking she could try to get under his skin like that. I—" She stopped with her hand on the doorknob and sighed. "She was a stupid girl whose head got too big for her own good. She got that from me. You don't threaten a man like that with going to the press about anything. You stay quiet."

Newbury felt like she wasn't talking to him anymore but he didn't stop her. "If I had stayed clean, I would have paid attention and stopped her before she—" Bell sighed. She sounded the saddest he thought he had heard anyone sound. Newbury turned his head back to the television. "I guess it looks like the two of you got the same knack for revenge. I'd tell you to be careful but you already know that's what got her killed." The door opened. The door closed.

He spent the rest of the night reading the text messages, the screenshots, the photos of contracts and NDAs. He didn't even process that he was holding the smoking gun. He read it like he would a news article or a book, back when he was in that apartment and he could stare at a screen long enough without feeling like his hair was made out of fine-tipped wires shoved directly into his brain.

There was something about being sound in this way, where his chest physically hurt in a way it never had before. Sound in the way that he knew what to do and he knew how to organize all the information in his head.

Rehabilitation clinic COO William Fairchild, billboard boy with tan skin and florescent bulb teeth. He has everything because he takes everything. Under the table drug operation, rehab programs as a front/laundering scheme/help-you-sleep-at-night. Heroin, pills, sex trafficking. All the nasty stuff.

She, of course, confronted him over an email of all things about all of this.

    i have everything.

Screenshots, written statements, a recording of Rob saying something about finding a girl locked up in the basement of their country house when he drove his car down there one weekend to steal some booze. Evidence from various crime scenes pawned off on friends as charitable "gifts"—a nice car, a freshly laundered black wool coat, new Italian boots. None of this would hold up in court, but she didn't know that.

> *men like you are the reason this country is*
> *like this.*
> *it's what you deserve for trying to take my*
> *fucking baby.*
> *i'm going to the fucking police and then the*
> *press, i hope you rot in prison you fucking*
> *scumbag*

She had then sent a collection of photos that didn't make much sense.

But that was almost at the end, a few hours before she would be gone.

There was the beginning: First Girl had to meet Boy. So Girl meets Boy. Boy is rich and Girl lives in an abandoned house just outside of town with her mother who has spent the better part of the last eight years rolling in and out of Boy's father's rehab clinics. And maybe it was love or maybe the condom just broke and she was too scared to go to Canada to get the abortion—plus, COO William Fairchild fixed up the house now that a future grandchild was in the picture, legitimate or not.

Running water and electricity, sometimes even some food in the fridge. Scheduled a midwife to live in with Girl the closer to the due date she got. The midwife was mean and only spoke Russian. Or Polish. Or something like that. And she kept making Girl eat anchovies and told her in broken English that once they baby was born they would have to leave.

The Boy, Robert, the baby's father, was gentle with her at least. Called her sweet things, such sweet things, promised her a future of big houses and nice dresses and pearl earrings. Told her they had to keep things quiet because she was still technically dating one of his friends, after all, and they had to maintain appearances, just for now.

She was too smart to be that gullible, but he was kind to her in a way no one had ever been before. Called her such sweet things.

And then he disappeared, just like that. She seemed despondent, strings of blue little messages asking where he was, why he was ignoring her, why no one was home. Days would pass and she would ask the same questions. Days more, late into the night. Her messages went from blue to green, a clear sign that the phone on the other end was either disconnected or blocked. But she kept sending them anyway, like she was expecting the empty space to call back.

> *my water broke and i was so scared Rob*
> *i was so scared.*
> *the people your father sent to help tried to*
> *take our baby away*
> *i wouldn't let them.*
> *he's taken so much from me i w ont let him*
> *i wont*
> *she's the most beautiful thing I have ever seen.*

Atticus was the first one to get up.

"The eclipse is going to be over soon," he said. Newbury didn't even realize it had grown eerily dark. "That means Mr. Fairchild is gonna be home."

"Alright," Newbury said after looking at the documents in his lap a little longer. "Okay. I need you to do one last thing for me. Alright kid?"

"Okay."

"I need you to sit under that desk and put your hands over your face, like this, yeah?" Newbury pressed his fingers over his eyes, hesitating for a moment before inching his index and middle apart to look at Atticus through the space it made. The boy smiled and copied him. Newbury smiled too. "Yeah, perfect. Like that."

Newbury stood, holding the documents in one hand and gently guiding the boy under the desk by his shoulder with the other. "You're going to hear a gun go off a few times but it's gonna be okay. Alright? Don't move from right there until Dewey comes up here to get you."

He walked to the door.

"Where are you gonna go?" Atticus asked.

Newbury paused in the doorway for a moment before responding.

"I'm going to find my granddaughter."

"Is that what the papers are for?"

"Some of them, yeah."

"Okay," Atticus, hands still over his face, nodded. He was sitting with his forehead rested against his knees, curled under the desk. All Atticus saw was dark, but, around him, the light lifted in a supernatural way. Totality complete. "Okay."

Newbury nodded to himself and walked out of the room. He descended the stairs. He stopped half-way down and sat. He pointed the shotgun at the front door. He waited.

CARRABELLE, FRANKLIN COUNTY

———

The girl's house stayed just how everyone left it.

It stayed because it had a history to it, even through the rising tides and fan falls of moths that threw their tiny bodies against its porch lights out of pure dumb habit. It had housed people, yes. The girl, yes. But also the family of doves that roosted in the leftmost kitchen cabinet months after the last officers left the scene, when the worst of the gore had been neatly scooped up in plastic bags that then, just as neatly, disappeared like nothing ever happened at all.

The house, like most houses bordering Southern bodies of water, had a rotten smell to it. An old wood, no air conditioning, musk that called out to stray cats and dogs, a collection of opossums, birds of prey that waited in the uppermost branches of the magnolia tree outside for their next meal.

The teenagers resumed their drunken fireworks displays in due time, and the sparks would continually illuminate the yawning maws of its glassless windows. During those brief but glorious bursts of light, the features of the house looked most like a face. The windows, eyes. The front door an open, tired, mouth. The shingles a weathered but hearty skin that had withheld hurricanes and rot and the burrowing teeth of palm rats and termites and longhorn beetles. All of this illuminated by that turmoil of white, red, green.

In time, dust had moved like waves through its slouching frame. The moths threw their small bodies against the lantern of the wandering man who broke a window in order to crawl inside and hide from a storm. There he had found a mess of a house except for one pristine room, and in the room was a far older copy of a picture book his father used to read him. He fell asleep on the living room floor with it pressed against his chest. He left in the morning. He did not take the book with him, but it left a happy hollow feeling in his gut for a long time after.

Years after everyone forgot that sorry girl's name, a group of children set small fires in what used to be the bedroom. They went into the forest they weren't supposed to explore because they wanted to escape angry mothers and cruel older brothers. They went into the forest and then walked until they emerged in a clearing with a broken-down little house. One of the boys made his friend cry when he talked about how his daddy would shoot deer right around here. That they could be shot dead and strung up in a backyard like they did that doe last summer. The boy didn't mention that he stayed up the whole night crying, too, because when his daddy let him touch the crown of her pale brown head it was soft and warm still, like his mama's hands.

Years even after this, once the big men in tall buildings wearing expensive suits allowed the whole world to sink into its own bathwater, a man with tired eyes that smelled of sea salt and grease would lay one calloused hand against what used to be the frame for the front door. He would be in a boat, a broken down old dingy, unknowingly borrowed from a stranger on a dock not too far away from where he was then.

And he would drive it right up to where the swamp grass had begun to overtake the home completely. Now that the house had decided to begin its collapse into the earth, filled with snakes and a curdling heat and swampy water up to its very center, it felt closer to complete surrender than ever.

The man, who dreamed of oceans of oil and bright white pills and a pretty little baby who had her mother's eyes and his mother's nose, would then lean the upper half of his stray-dog body over the side of the boat to press his forehead into the frame. He would take a deep breath and whisper something simple yet delicate into the darkness inside. He would wait a moment and rub his thumb over a certain notch in the wood. He would never set foot inside.

And each of these moments pass by, as waves to a shore. The folded ghosts of cloth tucked neatly into drawers rot into nothing. Four of the little ceramic pots remain, stacked along the windowsill. They fill with water every time it rains, little bits of moss cling to their cracks and folds. The insects and the family of doves roosting in the leftmost kitchen cabinet caw into the dawn's empty orange. The fog rolls over the house and its quiet shoulders. The sycamores bristle at the winter wind's forceful chant.

And if one could listen hard enough—past the prisoners' songs that lurked like lonely ghosts, just over the collection of trees, past the crack and shutter of the overgrown magnolia, down and through the river's broad serpentine back—one would hear the breath of waves beating against salt-weathered rock. The sea, actualized. The crunch of ocean's grass, the caterwauling of gulls, the shift of sand under a mother's soft feet, and an ancient fog horn. There would always be the crackling of some radio, or child's song, or two voices harmonizing in imperfect laughter. This much is always true.

ACKNOWLEDGEMENTS

———

Thank you to my father, whose childhood stories were the inspiration for more than half of this book. Thank you to my mother, who has taught me the most important lesson of being true to myself. Thank you to Lissa, Teresa, and Cora, the second family I am forever thankful for, and all those stormy days on Nantucket that inspired me to continue writing no matter what.

Thank you to all my mentors at Poly: Virginia Dillon, Sarah Bates, Emily Gardiner. Thank you all for pushing me to always challenge myself no matter where I am. I would not have had the courage to do this if it weren't for you.

Thank you to *Bodega Magazine*, who first allowed me to give Atticus's voice a platform before this book was even a thought in my head. Thank you to all the amazing folks at New Degree Press for their incredible program. Without

Brian Bies, Eric Koester, and Kristy Carter this book would never have existed.

And thank you to everyone who pre-ordered the eBook, paperback, and multiple copies to make publishing possible, who helped spread the word about *Southing*, and who helped me publish a book I am proud of. I will be forever grateful for all of your love and support.

Garland M. Lasater*

Samuel Kory*

Jennifer Shultz*

Hoehn Matthias

James Anderson

Eden Rohrer

Svetlana Shlyam

Mo Rajji Courtney

Eva Zelig

Liat Weinstein

Sarah Bates

Jules Spector

Joella Waldman

Wickham Bermingham

Alejandra Sanchez

Rachel Green

Eric Koester

Alev Sibel Yorulmaz

Frederic Troadec*

Diana Calabrese

Sharon Dillon

Donna Muoio

Theresa Timmes*

Blake Moore

Kathryn Wright*

Cora Sangree

Kristen Kelch*

Daniel Doughty

Paul Pronio

Kraig Kuzirian*

Cathleen Lewis

Anne Tindell

Michelle Istakhorova

Dean Byington

Ana Tessier

Emily Gardiner

Ivy Trocco

Alexandre Davis*

Maddie Winter

Bessie Petroutsas

Linda Darling*

Joseph Santore

Gillian Sutliff

Sofiya Soboleva

Austin Tindell*

Maria Groom*

Virginia Dillon Bouillerot

Sarah Whalen

Sarah Nia

Cary Ng*

Brian O'Connell

Kris Percival

Serge E.

Thad Ziolkowski

Amy Joan Chew

Sammi Cohen

Key: *multiple copies/campaign contributions

Most of all, thank you Bryer. We're in this together.

www.ingramcontent.com/pod-product-compliance
Lightning Source LLC
Chambersburg PA
CBHW071524180526
45171CB00002B/365